The *Time-Saving Breakthrough*
that **Slims, Sculpts,** *and* **Builds**
the **Body** *of* **Your Dreams**.

The Miracle **SEVEN**

JOHN *e.* PETERSON
& Wendie Pett

*S*trength
& Honor

BRONZE
BOW PUB

The Miracle **SEVEN**

The *Transformetrics™ Training System* is a trademark that is the exclusive property of Bronze Bow Publishing Inc.

ISBN 1-932458-17-4

Published by Bronze Bow Publishing Inc.,

2600 E. 26th Street, Minneapolis, MN 55406

You can reach us on the Internet at www.bronzebowpublishing.com

Literary development and cover/interior design by Koechel Peterson & Associates, Inc., Minneapolis, Minnesota.

Manufactured in the United States of America

TABLE OF CONTENTS

Most people look in the mirror and would love to be in great shape. Not only because they would look so much better, but because they would also *feel* so much better. After all, what could be better than feeling energized and in love with life 24/7? In fact, let's be honest, being in great shape would allow us to gain the very most and achieve the very best from the life that God has given us.

So why doesn't everyone automatically make being in great shape a top lifelong priority? There are a multitude of reasons, but here's what Wendie and I hear the most. First, there's a fear that what it takes to get into great shape and then to maintain it will require too much time from their already over-committed schedules. Then there are the issues of the costs of buying exercise equipment or joining a gym and hiring a personal trainer, not to mention babysitters, the commute time, and on and on the list goes. Get the picture?

That's why "The Miracle Seven" is IDEAL! By following the Transformetrics™ Training System outlined here, Wendie and I will show you how to achieve the kind of strength, fitness, and vitality you have always dreamed of having. And you can do it without having to join a gym, buy expensive equipment, or waste a moment of your time doing anything that doesn't deliver a maximum return on your investment of time. Best of all, you won't be doing anything that will compromise your body, cause pain or injury, create overuse symptoms, or leave you feeling drained rather than energized.

You will start out by learning "The Miracle Seven Tiger Moves" as taught by martial arts legend John McSweeney. It is a system of exercise that is so natural, so simple, and so powerful that it actually heals the body as it energizes it to the max.

Then Wendie and I present seven separate daily workouts of seven exercises each that will help you sculpt, build, and strengthen every muscle of your body from your neck to your toes, evenly and naturally. And once again, all with no gym and no equipment.

Men, how would you like to build your arms, chest, and shoulders? How about giving your abs some definition, or building your legs, and maybe even create that V-shape back you've always wanted?

And, ladies, how would you like to give yourself an overall body lift as you slim and sculpt your arms, torso, abdomen, hips, buttocks, and legs and achieve a perfectly shaped dancer's body that moves with feline grace?

If you have answered YES! to any of these questions, you will find exactly what you need to achieve your goals with the Transformetrics™ Training System as presented here in "The Miracle Seven." What's more, we will also guide you with quick and easy-to-follow references to maximum nutrition so that you can speed your results and shed excess body fat on the hurry-up as those slim, beautifully shaped muscles become obvious in no time.

Wendie and I invite you to discover this and much, much more as you follow "The Miracle Seven" and Transformetrics™ to achieve the body of your dreams. And as Wendie says, "Dare to be transformed."

CHAPTER 1

YOUR BODY
A Masterpiece Waiting to Be Revealed

- Do you think your body is flawed?

- Do you think having a perfectly sculpted physique or figure is for someone else and not for you?

- If you answered yes to either of the above questions, then please read on because I have written this chapter just for you!

In my book *Pushing Yourself to Power*, I wrote a section outlining exactly what the seven attributes of dynamic strength and fitness include. They are: 1) strength, 2) flexibility, 3) endurance, 4) balance, 5) coordination, 6) speed, and 7) aesthetics. To illustrate this section I used a photo showing Michelangelo's masterpiece sculpture of King David.

Universally, Michelangelo's David has been revered as the highest manifestation of sculpture art since it was first revealed to the public in 1504. It was a project that Michelangelo began in 1501 at the age of 29, and one that the impassioned sculptor worked diligently at for three years in order to reveal the flawless physique of King David.

But consider this. That great block of Carrara marble that Michelangelo began sculpting in 1501 wasn't even considered to be of suitable grade. In fact, when the master first began to sculpt his colossal thirteen-foot tribute to King David, it wasn't just a secondhand hunk of stone. It was literally at least a thirdhand, discarded chunk of marble. Two other sculptors, Agustino di Duccio and Antonio Rossellino, had begun to work with this same exact piece of marble. Both gave up in disgust because as they said, "It was impossible to control the amount of stone that could be 'chipped' [chiseled] away." So both men in separate circumstances abandoned the stone, and there it sat discarded and alone to face the elements for more than 20 years in the courtyard of the Cathedral of Florence. Its sole purpose, a resting place for birds.

But then one day in 1501, young Michelangelo saw this forsaken block of marble. He stared at it as though in disbelief because he knew that underneath all the excess stone that simply needed to be chiseled away by the master's own hammer and chisel was the masterpiece he saw as clearly as if it were standing before him. Michelangelo saw David in his own mind's eye. And slowly but surely the masterpiece of manly perfection emerged from the stone under the watchful eye of the master himself, as Michelangelo himself put it, "The more the marble wastes, the more the statue grows." To this day, more than 500 years later, Michelangelo's David is still the model for manly perfection.

So how does this relate to you? Why have I taken the time to tell you this story and give you a lesson in art history? Because that discarded piece of stone may in fact represent you! It may well be that you have tried other methods of training. Methods that promised exceptional results that flat out didn't deliver. In fact, you may have tried other methods that left you exhausted, starving, and, even worse, injured. If that's the case, I can tell you that you're not alone. Millions of people have experienced exactly the same thing only to give up in disgust when the only thing that appeared to get thinner was their wallet!

That's where the Miracle Seven is totally different. You're not going to spend hours performing aerobics that have minimal body sculpting value. Nor will you be subjected to a rigorous weight training schedule that with the passing of time is almost guaranteed to have you suffering joint pain and compression of the lower spine. (I know because I receive hundreds of e-mails from busted-up weightlifters who have all told me that they wished they had discovered the Transformetrics™ Training System years sooner.)

How about countless repetitions of calisthenics? Forget that too! The right calisthenics can be valuable additions to your program if they are done correctly, but you won't be doing endless, senseless repetitions of anything. No, you won't be using weights, going to a gym, or using countless numbers of repetitions of anything to achieve your goals and the body of your dreams. Instead, you'll be using Transformetrics™, the world's best, most natural, and most efficient method of body transformation and physical sculpting ever developed.

So what will you be using? Your body! Created by God, the greatest sculptor of all, to give you the best, most complete, and safe system of natural bodybuilding ever created.

In fact, with Transformetrics™ you *are* your own gym. But before I tell you what Transformetrics™ is and why it is clearly superior to all other methods of body transformation, let's discuss the methods we won't be using and why.

Yes, the ancient Greeks understood physical perfection.

AEROBICS

I hear the thoughts already whizzing through your head: *You've got to be kidding. You can't be saying you're against aerobics. You'd have to be insane. Aerobics have been proven absolutely essential for good health, and you'd be going against solid, foundational medical science to say that aerobics are worthless. Right?* Well, yes and no.

Yes, aerobics are essential for all-around cardiovascular health, and there is more than ample evidence to support this scientific fact. But when it comes to body sculpting, forget it! Aerobic exercises definitely have their purpose, but body sculpting isn't one of them. Think I'm wrong? Okay, I'll tell you what. The next time you see a marathon being advertised, just go and watch the race objectively as an observer. While there, ask yourself, "How many lithe, sculpted bodies do I see?" Chances are *very few*, if any. In fact, if you're honest, you'll be surprised how many thin fat guys you'll see.

There goes your mind again. *What? Thin fat guys? C'mon, John, that's a contradiction in terms.* Although I freely admit that on the surface it does sound like a contradiction, I assure you that it most certainly is not! Just observe what you're seeing at the marathon race. At first glance you'll see a large number of men who on the surface look extremely thin, almost to the point of being gaunt, frail, and emaciated. But the closer you look, the more you'll see. Rarely will you see a marathoner with a "six pack." I know because I've run more than one marathon where I was literally the only guy who had a six pack.

Most often what you will see is skinny, scrawny-looking guys who have no chest, arms, or shoulders and have loose fat hanging on their pecs, abs, and lower back. Why? Because although they *may* be in superb cardiovascular health, they have done nothing to develop and sculpt the rest of their bodies, and sometimes it is painfully evident. Also, did you notice that I used the word "may" when I wrote they "*may* be in superb cardiovascular health." The truth is that there have been several documented cases of marathoners dying from cardiovascular disease. Even to the point of dying while either training or engaged in a marathon race.

In fact, that's exactly how author James Fixx, who wrote *The Complete Book of Running* that ignited the 1970s running boom, died. He literally died while on a training run at age 52. The same was true for Maryland Congressman Goodloe Byron, who died during a marathon race in 1978. When an autopsy was performed, it was determined that the congressman had been running marathons with arterial openings the "size of pin pricks." So, the bottom line is that although aerobics *may* dramatically improve cardiovascular fitness, the truth is aerobics by itself is no insurance policy. And besides that, there's no way that aerobics will give you a lithe, sculpted physique.

Please don't assume that I am negative on running or aerobics—I'm not! I personally average 3 to 5 miles daily and truly enjoy running outdoors in the fresh air. I just don't want you to make the mistake of thinking that it can sculpt you, because it flat out can't.

Now you're asking yourself, *So what about swimming?* Well, swimming is definitely terrific aerobic exercise as well, but if you're thinking that it will give you a nicely sculpted physique, think again. In *Pushing Yourself to Power*, I wrote about a marathon swimmer whom my buddy and I went to hear as well as participate in his "Ultimate Fitness" seminar. When this guy came out to speak, he looked a lot more like he had been training to play Jubba the Hut in the next installment of *Star Wars* than in swimming the English Channel or the Straits of Magellan as he lectured about. Literally, there was nothing about strength, fitness, or health we were going to learn from him. And as my friend Wayne said that night, "That guy didn't swim anywhere. He's so fat he just floated on the tide like a bar of soap."

So, although I think it's an excellent idea to perform 30 minutes of nonstop aerobic activity daily for cardiovascular health, it's not part of the Miracle Seven Body Sculpting Program because it flat out doesn't sculpt!

WEIGHT TRAINING

Okay, John and Wendie, are you telling me that you developed the physiques shown in these photos without ever following an intense weight program? C'mon now, I wasn't born yesterday.

Oh really? Well, what makes you think that weight training is the only way to build and sculpt a beautiful physique? In fact, what even remotely makes you think it's the best way?

Have you ever stopped to think about what "weight training" accomplishes? It doesn't matter whether we're talking about machines or free-weights. I'm talking specifically about what weight training accomplishes. Answer: It amplifies gravitational force in order to force your muscles to contract against resistance. That's it! Nothing more, nothing less. If you're using 20-pound dumbbells, you're working against 20 pounds of gravitational force. Thirty-pound dumbbells give you 30 pounds of gravitational force. And so on. That's all weight training does. It simply amplifies gravitational force to make the muscles contract. There's no magic to it.

The muscle contraction aspect is good, of course. But it's the side effects of weight training that definitely are bad. For instance, imagine that you are doing bicep curls with 30 pounds in each hand. At first, while your muscles are fresh, you can really feel the weight working the muscles. But after a few sets, your muscles are fatigued, and the resistance is being transferred from the muscles to the joints, tendons, and ligaments. Not only that, but you have also placed your spine under continuous compression because, after all, you've just added 60 pounds to the weight of your upper body. Over time, this amplified gravitational force literally squeezes the spinal fluid out of the spongy discs that separate your vertebrae, and this abusive treatment of your vertebrae will lead to bone rubbing against bone, causing tremendous pain because there is no longer any padding or cushioning to separate them. When that happens, all you have to look forward to is a life of chronic and debilitating pain and regular visits to a compassionate chiropractor.

But it doesn't end there. Take, for instance, the bench press exercise. There are literally tens of thousands of men and women suffering from torn rotator cuffs—sometimes in both shoulders—because of a preoccupation with this one exercise. In addition, there are tens of thousands suffering from bad elbows, bad wrists, severe lower back and knee pain, all of which are associated with bench pressing, dead lifts, and barbell squats. Does weightlifting build muscles? Sure it does. But it also destroys joints, ligaments, and tendons in the long term and is the source of chronic, debilitating, and lifelong pain. It has become so chronic that the *Wall Street Journal* ran a major feature on the disabilities and injuries caused by weight training in its March 13, 2003 edition.

So, what's the answer? Does one just accept pain and disability as the price one pays to have a muscular physique or figure? Is it inevitable, or is there another way? A way that delivers superb results while protecting joints, ligaments, tendons, and the muscles themselves. A way that is so natural it requires no gym and no equipment. A way that is so perfect that it can be practiced by virtually anyone, whether they're 9 or 99. The answer to that question is a very affirmative yes! And Transformetrics™ is the way!

NO WEIGHTS, NO GYM, NO PROBLEM!

Charles Atlas students developed fabulous physiques using nothing more than their own bodies. Below is a reprint of a Charles Atlas ad from 1937. I think it makes the point.

Photo courtesy of Sandow & the Golden Age of Iron Men

CHAPTER 2

SO WHAT IS *Trans*FORMETRICS?
the ultimate training system

Transformetrics™ is a system of exercises that incorporates four distinctly different forms of exercise into one cohesive whole. It allows you to achieve much the same muscle sculpting and bodybuilding benefits of weight training without any of the injuries and debilitating effects caused by weight training. In fact, many of our students and practitioners have verified repeatedly that they have actually witnessed dramatic improvements in both functional strength and muscle sculpting far beyond any other method they have ever tried, but without experiencing any of the pain and disability that occurs with long-term weight training.

Which brings up a point that has to be made:

All true strength, fitness, and health building exercise systems should prevent injury and accelerate healing. An exercise system should never be the source of pain and injury. If it is, it is doomed to fail! God only knows how many people have been injured because of so-called "expert advice."

TRANSFORMETRICS™

Transformetrics™ incorporates four distinct types of exercise into one cohesive, natural exercise system. These include Dynamic Visualized Resistance Exercises (DVR), Dynamic Self-Resistance Exercises (DSR), Isometric Contraction, and Power Calisthenics.

1. DYNAMIC VISUALIZED RESISTANCE EXERCISES (DVR)

Dynamic Visualized Resistance Exercises are so powerful in and of themselves that many of our Transformetrics™ practitioners focus almost exclusively on them alone. These exercises allow you to powerfully contract every muscle group from neck to toes and to achieve superior results that surpass almost every other form of exercise. This type of exercise has been used since ancient times and many yoga systems have used these types of exercises for bodybuilding purposes. The following is an excerpt from *Yoga and Health* by Selvarajan Yesudian and Elizabeth Haich that was published by Harper and Brothers in 1953.

"**The oldest muscle-building Indian 'Dhandal and Bhasky' exercises differ from western gymnastics primarily in that they do not consist of thoughtless repetitions but of exercises performed with great interest....We use our imagination to send vital force to various parts of the body, persistently developing strength, and if we watch our muscles during our exercises or watch them in a mirror, we will soon build a body so beautiful that even athletes will admire it.... All we need is a mirror and fifteen minutes every day. With the system of slow motion exercise, which prescribes no stultifying gymnastics but consists of movements like a game, combined with strong mental concentration, powerful muscles are developed within a very short time.**"

This same type of exercise program was also practiced by many of the old-time greats, including Charles Atlas, Earle E. Liederman, George Jowett, Maxick, and many others.

On more than one occasion martial arts legend John McSweeney told me that repetition-for-repetition no other form of exercise even came close to delivering the improvements and benefits in strength, physique building, and radiant health that resulted from following his *Tiger Moves* system of seven Dynamic Visualized Resistance Exercises. And if you have seen his photos, you know that McSweeney was his own best advertisement for the effectiveness of those seven exercises. When he was in his sixties and seventies, he had a powerful, athletic physique that made men a third of his age jealous. In addition, he could kick some serious butt and throw a looping overhand right with the same quality of raw power that I associated with a young Rocky Marciano. You didn't want to be on the receiving end.

So, it shouldn't surprise you that in the first section of this book on all-around health and strength building exercise that we feature John McSweeney's *Seven Tiger Move Exercises*. I guarantee that if you do nothing more than become an expert at the execution of these seven exercises alone that you can achieve levels of functional strength, power, and a flawless physique or figure that will be the source of untold compliments.

And yes, the seven DVR *Tiger Moves* that were taught by John McSweeney are in fact the *Miracle Seven*. More on that later.

2) DYNAMIC SELF-RESISTANCE EXERCISES (DSR)

In *Pushing Yourself to Power*, I told the complete story of how my grandfather and Uncle Wally put me on the Charles Atlas Dynamic Tension Training System when I was ten years old. A big component of the Atlas system included what I call Dynamic Self-Resistance Exercises (DSR). These exercises are a first cousin to the DVR exercises, which were also a part of the Atlas system, and allow you to contract with maximal force as you use one limb or muscle group to resist another. Once you learn the mind/muscle connection necessary to implement these exercises, you will be amazed at how you can isolate and sculpt every muscle from your neck to your toes.

In addition to the obvious benefits they present, all the DSR exercises can be made into isometric contractions at virtually any point within a range of motion (see Liederman pectoral contraction photo). And truth to tell, no form of exercise is harder to do or delivers better results for strength and physique than isometric contractions when combined with DVR and DSR. As a testimony to that, I have pictures of Charles Atlas on the beach at age 75, showing such a flawless physique that it's obvious why he had such a big smile (which, by the way, was an Atlas trademark). I know a lot of twenty-year-old men today who would give their "eye teeth" to have his physique.

So, in addition to DVR exercises we will also be practicing DSR exercises. You will note later on that we use many DSR exercises when we get to the daily body sculpting lessons. And as you will witness, these exercises are superb for strengthening, shaping, building, and sculpting every part of the body.

Liederman Pectoral Contraction: *works biceps, triceps, and pectorals.*

3) ISOMETRIC CONTRACTION

The first time I saw an isometric contraction properly performed was in July 1963, when I was ten years old. It was about a month after my grandfather and Uncle Wally took me under their wing and put me on the Charles Atlas Dynamic Tension Training System. The occasion was the annual family reunion, which was always a great time. And, of course, even though I had only been training for a month, Uncle Wally and Grandpa were already telling everyone about how much muscle I had built in only 30 days. (Nobody ever had anyone more affirmative in their life than my grandfather and Uncle Wally were for me. They were like two guardian angels. I hope some of you men realize what a profound impact you can have in a boy's life if you just take the time to notice and affirm them.)

The family reunion was a magical day. My dad and uncles were just getting going on their World War II stories when Uncle Milo showed up. Milo was the tallest of my uncles—he was 6'3" and weighed 210 pounds of the most perfectly sculpted muscle you could possible imagine. But somehow he looked different that day. Now keep in my mind that my grandfather had put all six of his sons on the Charles Atlas Training System as soon as they reached twelve years of age, *if not* sooner, and all the brothers had exceptional physiques. They literally looked like living, breathing Greek statues.

It was my dad who spoke up. "My gosh, Milo, what have you been doing? You look like someone carved you out of stone."

When I heard Dad say that, I did a double take. It was true. Uncle Milo's facial and neck muscles were even more obvious than usual, and his forearms were sheer cords of muscle.

"Well, Al," said Uncle Milo, "I started adding isometrics to my Dynamic Tension Exercises about four months ago, and everyone tells me that they can see a big difference."

Believe me, you could. Then all my uncles as well as my grandfather started talking about isometrics. As it turned out, Milo started practicing isometrics after he read an article about President Kennedy practicing them on the advice of the White House physicians. Milo reasoned that an isometric exercise was really a Charles Atlas self-resistance exercise where so much force was applied in both directions that no movement occurred because the muscles were involved in a deadlock wrestling match against each other for 10 seconds.

"Exactly how do you do that, Milo," my uncle Robert asked.

Uncle Milo stood up and took off his shirt. To this day I have never seen a more perfectly developed man. I've seen lots of guys with bigger arms, bigger chests, and bigger legs, but I've never seen one more perfectly put together than my uncle. In fact, if you've ever seen the physique of the actor Woody Strode, you know precisely what my uncle Milo looked like.

Well, Milo did a few self-resistance Atlas bicep exercises to warm his muscles up and then on the fourth rep, halfway up he performed an isometric contraction. With all his might, his left arm was pushing down while his right arm was pulling up. For 10 seconds his muscles looked as though they were involved in a life-or-death struggle. Far more than just a bicep isometric contraction, it appeared as though every muscle in his entire body was flexed to its absolute limit. Literally, every muscle fiber in his neck, pectorals, arms, abs, and back stood out in bold relief. It was an incredible demonstration of how to perform an isometric contraction correctly.

Alexander Zass *was a strong man during the 1920s famous for bending bars and breaking chains. He trained almost exclusively with Isometric Contraction.*

When Uncle Milo finished, my grandfather said, "That's how the strongman Zass trained. Same kind of exercises I read about years ago in *Physical Culture*, but I'd never actually seen it done until now."

Seriously, if you had seen my uncle perform that isometric contraction on that day, you'd never wonder whether or not isometric contraction is a valuable form of exercise. No, instead you'd be standing in line to buy the course and learn how to do it. In fact, that's exactly what I wanted to do. Later on in the day, I cornered my uncle Milo when he was talking with Grandpa and Wally and asked him if he would teach me isometrics. All three men laughed at my exuberance and desire to become strong.

Then Grandpa said, "I'm sure Uncle Milo will tell you that you should just concentrate hard on what you're already doing. You're only ten years old, Jackson, and you need to learn how all your muscles work and move before you start pushing them to the limit."

Seeing my obvious disappointment, Uncle Milo ruffled my hair and said, "Your grandpa's right, Jackson. I was thirty-eight before I ever did an isometric. But I'll tell you what: You remind me on your eighteenth birthday and I'll teach you personally." Long story short, I reminded him and he did!

Now, I want to verify one important point. Isometric contraction is singularly the best and most efficient method of dramatic strength and physique enhancement—period. However, it requires an absolute mind/muscle focus and is the single hardest exercise you can possibly do. It's true that an isometric contraction lasts only 7 to 10 seconds, but those are 7 to 10 seconds of the most intense and difficult exercise you will ever perform. Do they work? Like a dream. But you must master DVR and DSR before you will ever be capable of performing a real isometric contraction. Why? Because DVR and DSR teach you how to think into and powerfully contract any muscle group at will. Once you develop that mind/muscle connection to the max, you'll be ready to try isometrics. But before that, forget it. You'll only become disillusioned.

4) POWER CALISTHENICS

Power Calisthenics are a vital part of the Transformetrics™ Training System. They allow you to maximize your athletic abilities and enhance all attributes of true dynamic strength and athletic fitness. But not all calisthenics are of equal value. In the Transformetrics™ Training System, you won't find a single calisthenic exercise that is nothing more than a mere arm waving (sorry, Richard Simmons). No, in fact, you'll discover that some of these exercises could help you develop a flawless physique and exceptional strength and fitness all by themselves. However, when combined with DVR, DSR, and ISOs, the results are *amplified* beyond your greatest expectations. The Power Calisthenics we teach include multiple variations of push-ups (including extended range handstand push-ups for very advanced students), multiple variations of pull-ups, and a wide range of other specially selected exercises that, when performed as directed (DVR style), will give exceptional results in minimal time.

So, there you have it. The Transformetrics™ Training System incorporates all four of these exercise types just listed, and the result of synergy of these exercises, when taken together, far exceeds the sum total of their individual components. That said, let's take a look at the Miracle Seven: Seven exercises that will build and sculpt your body to its own natural perfection.

THE MIRACLE SEVEN
of John McSweeney

How would you like to learn seven exercises that require no gym and no equipment and yet are so result-producing that friends and loved ones will start asking you if you've been working out with a personal trainer? Not only that, but how would you like it if you could practice these same exercises virtually anytime and anyplace that you feel you have enough privacy? "What's the catch?" you ask. The catch is, *there is no catch.*

These seven exercises are the Seven Tiger Moves that I learned from John McSweeney. I mentioned John earlier when I was outlining the DVR Exercises. John McSweeney was a master of the martial arts. He was one of legendary Ed Parker's first martial arts students and became a superior martial artist, teacher, and friend to all who knew him. John was a veteran of three branches of the military, having served in the Navy during World War II, the Air Force during the Korean War, and later in the Army. He was also a prolific writer.

As an instructor/teacher, John refined his skills and instructions to the point that he taught "only the stuff that works," as he put it, and as a result there were no high, flashy kicks in the McSweeney Martial Arts System. Instead, John taught devastating strikes that he had personally developed from Kenpo Karate as well as the

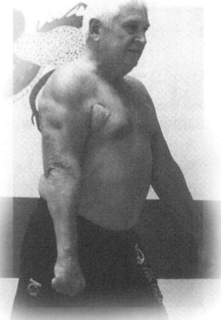

"At age 63 John McSweeney was his own best advertisement for the power of Tiger Moves."

JOHN E. PETERSON

Circular Power Strikes of Combat Kung Fu. John believed that if something, *anything* had no real-life application, then it was time to get rid of it. It didn't matter how long a certain technique had been a part of a tradition—if it didn't work, it wasn't part of the McSweeney System, period. The same was true of exercise.

John McSweeney had tried just about every system of exercise imaginable. He tried weightlifting, calisthenics, isometrics, yoga, Tai Chi, Qi Gong, and almost every other exercise discipline that has seen the light of day. But in terms of benefits in strength, physique development, and the acquisition of vibrant health, John was adamant—nothing compared to his system of Dynamic Visualized Resistance exercises that he called "Tiger Moves."

As McSweeney and I discussed them, I told him that I could clearly see the similarity between these exercises and the Dynamic Tension Exercises I had been practicing since I was a kid, and he agreed. But he added that even though he had done the Atlas exercises as a young man, he didn't

John McSweeney performing the "Barrel Squeeze," a.k.a. the "Full Range Pectoral Contraction."

believe they were as effective as his Tiger Moves. So I asked him why he thought that was the case—not that I didn't believe him, but I wanted to hear it from the master himself.

McSweeney said, "It doesn't matter whether you're talking about Charles Atlas, Earle Liederman, or any of the great mail-order instructors of the past. They all had good information, but they never taught anyone the essential key of how to gain the most from their respective systems of exercise. That key was how to think into and powerfully contract every muscle group at will. Without this specific understanding, you're missing the greatest benefit completely. On the other hand, once you learn this 'secret,' you're free! You will never need to rely on weights again, or high repetitions of calisthenics, or anything else that ultimately causes far more harm than any amount of benefit to the body's structure."

When I heard his explanation, I knew he was absolutely correct. But he didn't stop there. He went on to say, "If Charles Atlas had taught this one specific detail so that his students had learned how to apply it to each and every exercise he taught, he would have had the ultimate training system for all time!"

I remember listening very intently to his words and then learning exactly how to perform each of the seven Tiger Moves while performing them in front of a mirror. As good a shape as I was in, I was surprised by the results when I followed through on exactly what John had taught me and performed the Tiger Moves exclusively for a period of three months along with my normal martial arts training. Before the end of those three months, people were telling me that my physique looked better than ever. And get this: I had not done a single push-up or pull-up in that entire time. All I did was the seven Tiger Moves of John McSweeney, and the results more than spoke for themselves.

Fast forward. Today, fourteen years later, I want to teach you these same exact Tiger Moves. I assure you that if you apply yourself to their performance each and every day for the next three months, you will be awed by the dramatic improvements in your physique/figure and all-around athletic fitness. Not only that, but if you are currently among the large numbers of people who have been injured through exercise, the Tiger Moves can go a long way toward helping you achieve dynamic, pain-free mobility.

In fact, now I'd like to introduce you to one of the most beautiful and fittest people whom I know, my friend and coauthor as well as the author of *Every Woman's Guide to Personal Power*, Wendie Pett. I'll let Wendie tell you her personal story about the effectiveness of Tiger Moves, and then I will rejoin her in teaching and demonstrating the Miracle Seven Tiger Moves of John McSweeney for you.

CHAPTER 4

THE MIRACLE SEVEN
for Women

As I reflect on how and why I became involved with Transformetrics™, the first image that comes to my mind is that of an extraordinarily active woman. She is determined and persistent and positive, but if you knew what to look for you would see the signs of disappointment and discouragement, and you would feel the wearying sense of rush that engulfs her every move. She's a working mom and wife who is striving to be in the best physical shape she can attain through aerobics, kickboxing, body pump, and even a personal trainer…only to find momentary satisfaction with each workout. No matter what training regimen is taken, the desired strength levels and body sculpting never materialize as she hoped. The prescription for the exact figure she had been trying to create for years never emerged…until she started training the Transformetrics™ way.

I, of course, am that woman, and Transformetrics™ is the one and only system that brought me quality over quantity and offered a method of training that delivered the exact results I was searching for without having to climb the barbell ladder I'd been told was the only way.

Thankfully, due to a horrible snowmobile accident (yes, I said thankfully) I was lured into trying Transformetrics™ as a way to help heal my injuries. Little did I realize that I would also learn how to become stronger, more sculpted, and more lithe than ever. Even though I had known John Peterson for several years and he had shared with me his "secrets" about how he achieved his strong, sculpted physique naturally, I was probably his biggest skeptic. John is 50+ and very well developed, and I had never met a man or woman in such phenomenal shape who didn't lift heavy weights or take an enhancement drug of some kind. Matter of fact, people ask John all the time if he takes steroids. Usually John responds with laughter in his voice, "If I did, I would be huge! Oh, not to mention I would probably be six feet under the ground, too."

Shortly after my accident and in desperation to dance in a competition that was three months off, I asked John to teach me his training technique. The shoulder injury I sustained in the accident (a broken clavicle) was both painful and frustrating, as I was normally very active. My three-year-old son was very active as well and needed me to be healthy and attentive. When I visited the orthopedic specialist, he said that the recovery time would be a few months, and I should forget about the dance competition. I knew I had to try something to jump-start the healing process. Transformetrics™ was my only trump card.

In my book, *Every Woman's Guide to Personal Power*, I wrote about getting fit for overall functional fitness. When I mentioned I was active, I meant that not only in the athletic sense of the word but with everyday activities as well. Whether it is running and playing with my son, planting my garden, doing chores around the house, or just carrying a heavy bag of groceries, I feel that nothing is more satisfying than being capable of accomplishing these tasks with ease. When a woman shows signs of strength in a feminine way, I believe she feels more confident and sexy. Look at women of the ancient times such as Venus de Milo. Her physique is

one that we look at and notice how functional and "real" her chiseled shape represents. Although her sculptor is unknown, Venus de Milo is one of the most famous ladies in the world and offers a feline grace that women desire to attain. Her curves are a masterpiece and distinguish the feminine beauty and attraction that men and women alike feel are pleasing to the eye.

The first exercises that John Peterson taught me to help heal my injuries quickly and effectively were the seven Tiger Moves. The McSweeney High Reach was my favorite move as I started noticing results in my overall strength as well as the day-by-day improvement of my injured shoulder. Almost immediately I noticed striations in my shoulder muscles that had never been visible before. As I trained with only the Tiger Moves in the beginning, I noticed I was shedding fat and replacing it with muscle everywhere—in my arms, abdomen, glutes, and legs. I remember thinking, *This seems way too easy, but it works! I think I've found the fountain of youth!* My friends started asking me what I was doing to recuperate so quickly and to develop such a sleek figure. I now have those friends on our program, and they are thanking me for their newly found physiques.

Granted, Transformetrics™ is a lifestyle change, and diet is the other change that needs to take place for maximum results. I found that once I started eating healthy along with Transformetrics™, the two lifestyle changes worked powerfully together. In fact, have you ever wondered what causes you to eat unhealthy, fatty foods in the first place? Yes, stress is a huge factor, but there's a physical element that comes into play. When you choose to eat fatty foods, a brain hormone called *galanin* is produced. This negative hormone regulates your desire for fat. The more fatty foods you eat, the more *galanin* your brain produces, increasing your desire for fatty foods even more. It's one big vicious circle. The secret is to eat balanced nutritious meals and treat yourself to fatty foods only on occasion. You are human, after all.

In a world that is obsessed with looking and feeling healthy and that caters to diminishing cellulite, I can't think of another program that accomplishes this in less time, with no required gym or equipment, and zero chance of incurring an injury. As a busy wife, mom, and full-time career woman, I personally relish its flexibility for my hectic lifestyle. Life is filled with choices, and how you spend your time and energy is up to you. Doesn't it make sense to accomplish your health goals in the most effective way possible so you can spend the rest of your time with family, friends, or doing something on your own that you enjoy?

Transformetrics™ is the best way to enhance and develop your God-given body to its fullest potential. Your body is a gift from God that keeps on giving if you treat it right. So why not treat it with respect?

John and I look forward to showing you the way to a new you in the next few chapters based on the seven Tiger Moves. We want you to be the best "you" that you can be, so, yes, *dare to be transformed!*

CHAPTER 5

ORIGIN OF THE MIRACLE SEVEN
Tiger Moves

Now that you've read Wendie's incredible story, you clearly understand that Tiger Moves are everything I have said they are. They are the perfect exercise system for men and women of all ages. Repetition for repetition, they deliver more benefits than virtually any other form of exercise. And while they can certainly build a powerful and beautifully developed physique or figure, they do so without any of the usual joint and tendon injuries associated with heavy weightlifting. But even more importantly, they accelerate healing while dramatically slowing the aging process. This is due mainly to the fact that Tiger Moves teach you how to conserve and powerfully use nerve force to your best advantage. As stated previously, weightlifting causes severe compression of the lower spine; this in turn inhibits the flow of nerve force not only to the muscles but also to all the vital organs of the body. As a result, premature aging is accelerated through the use of excessively heavy weights.

When I first contacted John McSweeney, he was 63 years old. Upon a closer look, I have never seen another 63-year-old man quite like him. He looked a lot closer to 45 than he was to 63, and he literally moved like an athlete of 25. What was more, he said he expected to stay that way right up to the end of his days, which was exactly what he did.

ANIMAL WISDOM

The first thing that McSweeney stated about his exercise system was that it was completely natural. He would then tell you that most of the conventional exercise systems actually caused far more pain and injury than benefit. He was quick to point out that exercise machines and free-weights can tear muscles, wear out joints, and do damage to the vascular system because of extreme fluctuations in blood pressure. He also stated that both jogging and long-distance running can injure bones, tendons, ligaments, and joints in the feet, legs, and lower back. He believed that running long distances (beyond five miles) expended energy needlessly, often in excess of the body's ability to recuperate. More to the point, he was adamant that too much of these wrong methods of exercise could make you look far older than your years!

By way of contrast, McSweeney talked about how tigers and other animals instinctively used a method of exercise that kept them in top shape throughout life, did no harm to their bodies, and kept them young right up to the time that death came to take them (sounds like a description of John himself). John told me in no uncertain terms that human beings would be far better off if they discarded the exercise methods they were taught and embraced the simple, instinctual exercise systems of tigers and other animals.

This was singularly the reason John called his exercises "Tiger Moves." He stated that Tiger Moves can produce a beautiful, well-proportioned physique for a man or woman, resembling that of a trained gymnast, as well as great strength and vibrant health. John also believed that the movements *energize* the body, which I can personally attest to having experienced, as well as fight the aging process by increasing blood flow throughout the smallest capillaries, including those located in facial skin. One of his moves, the High Reach, "has curative powers," McSweeney told me, "and can restore an injured shoulder to its normal range of motion." If you doubt his veracity, Wendie and I suggest you immediately visit the www.bronzebowpublishing.com forum and read how it has been verified hundreds of times by forum members. (We also invite you to become a member today.)

McSweeney went on to say (as though I wasn't already sold just by looking at him), "They require no gym and no equipment and can be done anywhere and anytime. They are far superior to weights, machines, or calisthenics, and I'm the living proof of their effectiveness."

GREAT TENSION

"So, what is my system?" McSweeney asked rhetorically. "Nothing more than contracting and extending your muscles with great tension while you are thinking into them. It's this mind/muscle connection that is absolutely essential. Have you ever watched a tiger or lion at the zoo? Ever watch him get up from a nap or change positions?"

"Sure I have, John," I answered. "Why?"

"Because the kind of exercise I'm talking about is exactly the same kind of exercise that tigers and lions perform every time they get up from a nap or change positions. They stretch their entire body with a tension so great that their limbs actually quiver. It's nothing like a man's yawning stretch or a static stretch to increase flexibility. The tiger's stretch is so powerful that it actually builds incredible strength and muscle; so much so that a tiger could literally tear the head right off a man. It's the tension that is the secret! The inner resistance produced by the tension builds muscle fibers just as much as the external resistance produced by weights or machines. However, since the resistance is perfectly controlled at all times throughout the entire range of motion, there is no jerking, no compression, and no harm done to the body."

LEARNING FROM THE ANCIENTS

In ancient Greece, physical culture was at its zenith. This is clearly evidenced when you visit a museum of antiquities and view sculpture that was created by the ancient Greek sculptors. These people knew precisely how to develop strength and perfectly sculpted bodies. How do you suppose they did this? They trained their bodies to become strong sculpted masterpieces without any of the body pump classes or the newest pieces of training equipment of today. They used power calisthenics including push-ups and pull-ups as well as controlled, super slow, resistance types of movements similar to those of Tiger Moves. And the same was also true of the ancient martial artists of India, China, and Mongolia. These people observed animals to learn fighting methods, which they incorporated into their martial arts systems. They also noted the animals' exercise methods and imitated them in tension exercises. The result was incredible power.

It was this component of his martial arts training that McSweeney began in 1960 that captivated him. Not only did he enjoy its fighting efficiency, but also its bodybuilding power. In fact, he was quick to point out that it wasn't long before the DVR tension exercises completely replaced the Atlas Power Calisthenics that previously kept his body muscular and strong. Still, something wasn't quite right. So, after a period of self-experimentation, McSweeney altered the ancient exercises, which had a limited range of motion, and changed them to movements that covered a full range of motion. This alteration allowed for *complete* contraction and expansion of the opposing muscle structures. The Seven Tiger Move DVR exercises were the end result of his experimentation.

Originally sculpted by Lysippos in 320 B.C., the Farnese Hercules shows a level of development not surpassed to this day.

GETTING THE MOST BENEFIT

To get the most benefit from *The Miracle Seven Tiger Moves*, consider the following:

■ **Aerobic Additions:** The Miracle Seven keep the entire body in great shape. But Wendie and I also recommend adding long walks, swimming, running up to 3 miles, or performing up to 300 to 500 Furey Squats several times each week.

■ **Frequency:** The Miracle Seven are the perfect exercise system. For the first few months Wendie and I both recommend that you perform 3 sets of 10 repetitions at moderate intensity. On a daily basis many friends who are now BronzeBowPublishing.com forum members have told us repeatedly how amazed they were because of how quickly they saw increases in muscle size and definition.

■ **Tension:** As stated repeatedly, the key to the system is the amount of tension used while performing each exercise. Vary the amount of tension until it feels comfortable. If you use only moderate tension, you will maintain muscle tone, but not dramatically increase the size of the muscles. If you use higher amounts of tension, you will perform fewer sets and repetitions as is indicated in the chart below. A sufficient amount of tension builds muscle fiber every bit as much as weight training but sculpts the bodies of men and women so that the body takes on the contours of a trained gymnast or in some cases, as Wendie has been told, "that of a jungle cat." In other words, lithe, flexible, beautifully sculpted, and very lean.

■ **Breathing:** The Miracle Seven should be performed slowly with great tension. Breathe using both the nose and mouth, inhaling on the way back or up and exhaling on the way forward or down. Don't be afraid to breathe.

REPETITIONS		SETS
MODERATE	8-10	3 max
HEAVY	6-8	2-3 max
VERY HEAVY	3-5	2 max

The Miracle SEVEN

Tiger Move EXERCISES

Foundational

Strength and

Fitness for Life

THE MIRACLE SEVEN
Tiger Move Exercises

The following exercise system includes seven Dynamic Visualized Resistance exercises. It is highly recommended that you perform them unclothed (whenever possible) in front of a large mirror. This allows for immediate feedback as you flex and contract your muscles at various levels of tension. By doing so you will literally see and learn how muscles look and feel at various levels of intensity.

The seven exercises are:

1. **FULL RANGE PECTORAL CONTRACTIONS**
2. **THE SHOULDER ROLL (DELTOID CONTRACTION)**
3. **THE WRIST TWIST (TRICEPS CONTRACTION)**
4. **McSWEENEY HIGH REACH**
5. **ONE ARM CHIN**
6. **ABDOMINAL CONTRACTION**
7. **HALF KNEE BEND**

Please read all descriptions carefully and follow the photographed sequence. Also, Wendie and I encourage you to stop by on our web site at www.bronzebowpublishing.com and view the exercises shown in video clip sequence. I demonstrate the exercises for the men, and Wendie demonstrates for the women.

FULL RANGE PECTORAL CONTRACTION

PRIMARY FOCUS: CHEST

STEP 1

Stand with your left foot about a pace forward. Left knee is bent and back is straight. Hold your hands facing each other just a couple inches apart. Powerfully flex all the muscles of the arms, shoulders, chest, and upper back before movement begins.

STEP 2

Bring your hands back slowly under great tension and continue until the back muscles are fully flexed. Hold this position for a count of "one tiger one."

STEP 3

While maintaining tension in the muscles, slowly move your hands forward until they are facing each other once again just a couple inches apart. Hold this position for a count of "one tiger one," then repeat the entire sequences for 9 more repetitions.

☞ Points to Remember:

■ Be sure your arms remain parallel to the floor throughout the entire range of motion.

■ Shoulders should be held naturally and not lifted.

■ Using both your nose and mouth, breathe *in* on the way back and *out* on the way forward.

tiger move

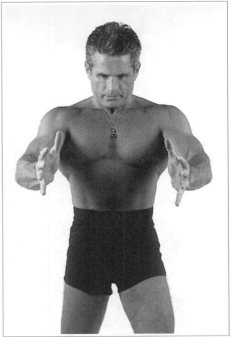

SHOULDER ROLL
PRIMARY FOCUS: DELTOIDS

STEP 1

Stand with your right foot forward about one pace. Your right knee is bent and your back is straight.

STEP 2

Start with your arms bent and hands in fists. Powerfully flex all the muscles of your forearms, biceps, triceps, pectorals, and deltoids before movement begins.

STEP 3

While maintaining tension in the muscles, slowly move your arms back with your forearms remaining parallel to the floor throughout the entire range of motion until the back muscles are powerfully flexed. Hold this position for a count of "one tiger one."

STEP 4

Return to the starting position by simply reversing the motion and retracing the exact same plane of motion. Repeat the entire sequences smoothly and fluidly for 9 more repetitions.

☞ Points to Remember:

■ Forearms remain parallel to the floor throughout the entire range of motion.

■ Shoulders remain low and not lifted.

■ Using both your nose and mouth, breathe *in* on the way back and *out* on the way forward.

tiger move 2

WRIST TWIST

STEP 1

Stand with your left foot one pace forward. Left knee bent, back straight, arms in front close to your body with fists turned in. Back of hands almost touching.

STEP 2

Powerfully flex the muscles of your forearms, upper arms, pectorals, and shoulders. While maintaining tension, slowly rotate your arms back, turning the fists gradually until they turn out. Flex your back muscles and triceps powerfully for a count of "one tiger one."

STEP 3

While maintaining tension slowly rotate your arms forward to starting position while turning your fists gradually until the backs of your hands are almost touching.

☞ Points to Remember:

■ Keep your arms pointing down throughout the entire range of motion.

■ This exercise works the triceps with great intensity but also works the deltoids and pectorals.

■ Keep movement smooth from beginning to end.

tiger move 3

McSWEENEY HIGH REACH

STEP 1

Stand with your feet shoulder-width apart.

STEP 2

Begin with both arms at shoulder height. With your right arm slowly reach as high as possible with great tension. As your right arm comes down to your shoulder, your left arm is reaching up with great tension.

STEP 3

Continue through 10 reps with each arm.

☞ Points to Remember:

■ Arms move independently under great tension in both directions.

■ Reach as high as is comfortably possible.

■ This is the movement that John McSweeney believed to have curative powers. Many of the BronzeBowPublishing.com Forum members agree and have used it to restore full mobility to injured shoulders.

tiger move 4

"This is the exercise that rehabilitated my shoulder!" - Wendie Pett

ONE ARM CHIN

STEP 1

Stand with your feet side by side and shoulder-width apart. Your left arm is above your head, your right arm at shoulder level.

STEP 2

While exerting great tension in the forearms and biceps of both arms, slowly start to pull your left arm down while moving your right arm to the "up" position.

STEP 3

As each arm comes down, bring them as close to the center line of the body as possible.

☞ Points to Remember:

■ Maintaining tension in both directions.

■ Come down the center line of the body as much as possible.

■ This exercise builds and strengthens biceps, forearms, inner pectorals, and especially the latissimis dorsi of the upper back for that classic V-shape.

• • • • •

One of our students from Boulder, Colorado, used this exercise exclusively to improve his pulling strength and went from a maximum of 4 pull-ups to 10 in just a matter of weeks. Bottom line: This is a powerful strengthener and V-builder.

tiger move 5

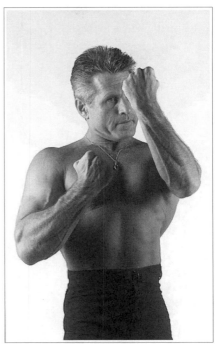

ABDOMINAL CONTRACTION

STEP 1

Stand with your feet side by side and shoulder-width apart. Arms in position shown, performing the Liederman chest press.

STEP 2

Press your abdomen down as hard as possible with great tension as you exhale powerfully. Hold for "one tiger one."

STEP 3

While inhaling to the maximum, consciously try to draw your abdomen in and up and try to feel as though it is touching the spine. At the point of greatest contraction, hold for "one tiger one."

☞ Points to Remember:

■ This is a great energizing exercise that can be performed anytime during the day.

■ It improves both digestion and elimination.

■ John McSweeney once told me that he had seen several people whom he knew lose several inches from their abdomens by learning how to powerfully contract both the "down" and "up" positions as indicated with this exercise.

■ This is also a great breath control exercise.

tiger move 6

HALF KNEE BEND

STEP 1

Stand with your feet side by side. Arms as shown, performing the Liederman Chest Press contraction.

STEP 2

While thinking into your leg (thigh) muscles and powerfully contracting them, slowly bend your knees and descend only halfway while maintaining maximum muscle tension.

STEP 3

Slowly reverse direction and come back up to the starting position while maintaining tension in upper body and legs.

☞ Points to Remember:

■ By maintaining an aerobic Isometric contraction of the upper body muscles (approximately 50 percent of maximum perceived effort), you will discover that it is much easier to contract the thigh muscles (quadriceps) very powerfully.

■ Breathe deeply, exhaling while going down and inhaling while coming up.

■ No need to go deeper than halfway unless you want to. But be careful not to harm the knee joint.

tiger move 7

CLOSING WORDS ON
*The Miracle*SEVEN TIGER MOVES

Working out with Tiger Moves will require approximately 15 to 20 minutes if you are practicing 3 sets of 10 repetitions at moderate intensity. If you are using great tension, follow the information on the chart provided to adjust both sets and repetitions. It is not recommended to do more than one ultra high-tension workout every 4 days and no more than 2 sets maximum of 3 to 5 repetitions. Remember, the more intense the contraction, the slower the movement. You may practice (in fact, it is recommended) Tiger Moves every day. But vary the levels of contraction to achieve the most benefit. Remember to breathe deeply at all times!

REPETITIONS		SETS
MODERATE	8-10	3 max
HEAVY	6-8	2-3 max
VERY HEAVY	3-5	2 max

Working out with The Miracle Seven Tiger Moves will result in a dramatic increase in both strength and lean muscle mass as you shed pounds of unwanted body fat. Your body will take on the contours of vibrant youth and stay that way through the years with only minimal effort. You'll never need a gym or exercise equipment, and in just 15 to 20 minutes each day you'll stay strong, healthy, and youthful.

If you have any questions, Wendie and I invite you to come to our web site at www.BronzeBowPublishing.com, and there you can view video clips of both Wendie and myself performing the Tiger Moves as well as the exercises found in this book. Thanks for joining us.

Now in the section of the book that follows, Wendie and I will give you seven complete workouts to build and sculpt every part of your body on the hurry up. These workouts have been especially designed to help you address the trouble spots you may not be pleased with. With the exception of Workout #5, which emphasizes pull-up/chin-ups, no equipment of any kind is required. As stated previously, you can achieve superb results with Tiger Moves alone. But some of you want enhanced strength and body sculpting in specific areas of your body, and these routines in combination with the Tiger Moves can amplify those results.

However, before we get to the body sculpting workouts, we need to address the subject of Nutrition. Bottom line: You can exercise until "frogs grow feathers" (as Uncle Wally used to say), but if you don't get your nutritional needs squared away, you'll never achieve the results you could have if they were. With that in mind, the next chapter takes you through a comprehensive nutrition plan that will dramatically enhance and speed your results and help you achieve the body of your dreams.

The Miracle**SEVEN**

Seven Miracle Steps to
NUTRITIONAL
Transformation

Awareness

Self-Control

Question

Be Consistent

Hydrate Yourself

Supplement Your Diet

Refrain

SEVEN MIRACLE STEPS
to Nutritional Transformation

1. *Awareness.* From now on it's important that you are aware of the nutritional value of the foods you choose to eat. In general, if you avoid eating foods that are processed and contain high concentrations of sugar and fat, you take a huge step toward achieving a lean, sculpted body.

2. *Self-Control.* From now on you will eat only until you are satisfied and not until you are full. For many people this requires a complete reeducation of personal nutrition habits. But once you are aware of this distinction you will be on your way to the lean, muscular physique you have always wanted.

3. *Question.* When dining out don't be afraid to be specific when asking your server about what a particular dish contains or how it is prepared. Learn to identify the hidden fat terms. "Lightly breaded" may mean "submerged in a tub of butter." Doing so can help you avoid hidden calories. And don't be afraid to ask for special preparations of menu items to reduce the fat.

4. *Be Consistent.* Several small meals as opposed to three large meals a day allow your body to process the food you eat much more efficiently while avoiding hunger or overeating at any given time.

5. *Hydrate Yourself* by drinking pure water. Depending upon your size, you'll need to drink at least 2 to 4 liters per day to obtain maximum benefit.

6. *Supplement Your Diet.* Because of the quality of our foods, it's difficult to get all the vitamins and minerals your body needs from the foods you eat. At the minimum, supplement your diet with a good food-based multivitamin to ensure you get all the nutrients you need.

7. *Refrain* from eating the wrong foods or at the wrong times. Your goal is to fuel your body with the best possible nutrients.

Let's Start Right...

Our goal is to change the ratio of lean muscle mass to stored body fat. But that does not necessarily mean "losing weight." In fact, I've worked with many people who gain 5 to 10 pounds of muscle while dropping inches from their waistline, hips, or buttocks. So don't concern yourself with what the scale says. In truth, all a scale does is measure the gravitational pull your body exerts to good old planet Earth. It tells you nothing about body density or the ratio of lean muscle mass to stored body fat.

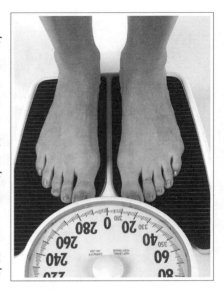

And don't for one moment believe those ridiculous ads that promise 10 pounds of "weight loss" over the course of a weekend. The only way that is possible is for you to take strong diuretics and lose water weight. Even if you did lose one or two pounds of fat by severely reducing your calorie intake, the rest of the loss would be water, and just as soon as you start rehydrating yourself the weight will come back on, but with an important difference. *If you lose weight by starving yourself, your body automatically slows down its metabolism (the rate at which your body consumes energy or calories).* When that happens, you literally set yourself up to store body fat at a much faster rate when you go back to normal food consumption. And the truth is, this could easily cause you to gain more fat than when you started...the exact opposite of the goal you want to achieve.

Lean, Strong, and Sculpted

Smart nutrition allows us to consume delicious, satisfying foods that provide our bodies with all it needs to maintain and build muscle tissue while simultaneously losing body fat. In fact, it is imperative that you eat enough high quality food and take high quality nutritional supplements in order to gain the most benefit from The Miracle Seven and the

Transformetrics™ Training System. The solution is simple: *Eat the right food at the right time, and your body will become a finely tuned fat burning machine that will make you leaner and healthier overall.*

There is no *dieting* or *diet* involved. Instead, what Wendie and I are presenting is a positive lifestyle change. The bonus for implementing these changes includes not only a well-defined muscular physique but greatly improved health. Your cholesterol level will go down along with your blood pressure, while your energy level goes up. And this will happen *without* the sacrifice of delicious food. The only foods you will be giving up are unhealthy combinations of refined fats and carbohydrates (sugars). But before you learn how to eat for a lean, muscular, and sculpted look, take a quick course on the basics of good nutrition.

Calories

We've all heard or read the term *calories*. For instance, a 20-ounce bottle of Coca Cola has 250 calories, according to the nutritional information on the label (which you need to check regularly). Why is that a big deal? Isn't a calorie just a calorie, after all? No. You need to look closer. According to the label, those 250 calories are comprised solely of sugar (carbohydrates)—*more than 60 grams of sugar!* More on that later.

Here's what you need to understand about food consumption. A calorie is simply a unit that measures the amount of energy required to raise the temperature of a gram of water by 1°C. All food contains energy (calories) or potential fuel for the body to operate and perform its many functions. Not unlike a car that will not operate without proper fuel, your body will not function properly if you don't eat. In fact, given enough time and a complete lack of food (fuel), your body will eventually starve to death. However, although an intake of "good" calories is absolutely essential for strength and fitness, not all calories are of equal value, and there are some calories you would be better off to avoid completely.

Here's why you need to discriminate in your calorie intake. The food you eat is divided into three basic categories—fats, proteins, and carbohydrates. Of the three, fats contain more than twice the number of calories per gram of either protein or carbohydrates. A gram of fat contains 9 calories whereas a gram of carbohydrate or protein supplies only 4 calories. In other words, 1 gram of fat at 9 calories contains more calories than 1 gram of protein and 1 gram of carbohydrate combined, which together equals only 8 calories.

But that's not the end of the "fatness" of fat calories. In one sense, fat calories really go straight to the waistline. This is true because it takes little or no energy for your body to digest fats. Only about 3 percent of the energy created by fat calories is used in the digestion process. This is also true with refined sugars. By comparison, it takes a great deal more energy to digest either protein or unrefined complex carbohydrate calories. In fact, laboratory studies have proven that it requires about 15 percent of the calories from either proteins or unrefined complex carbohydrates just to complete the digestion process. Simply put, when you consume fat or sugars (refined carbohydrates), you're feeding your body calories that require almost no digestion at all. And since most of us don't make our living by climbing mountains, these refined calories are immediately available for storage at their favorite fat storage sites on your body. This is not a good thing.

Protein

Unless you've been living in a cave for the last few years, you're aware that protein is your friend in the quest for a lithe, muscular, sculpted body. And Wendie and I don't dispute this because it's absolutely

true—especially when you consider that most of your body material is composed of protein! Muscle, internal organs, blood, hair, and even your fingernails are all composed of protein. In addition, protein also plays a major role in regulating water balance throughout your body. Important? You bet.

First, we need to define protein. Protein are large, complex molecules composed of 22 amino acids. Eight of the amino acids are produced by the human body, but the other 14 "essential amino acids" are not and must be obtained from foods that contain them. The foods that contain all 14 essential amino acids are red meats, poultry, fish, milk and milk products, and eggs. The problem with relying solely on these sources of complete protein is that some of these products are also very high in fat (with the exception of egg whites).

So although these foods are excellent sources of protein, we recommend that you obtain your protein requirements for the most part from low-fat sources, such as the white meat of chickens and turkeys, ultra lean meats such as wild game, buffalo, and lamb, fish of all types, low-fat dairy products, and egg whites. In addition, there are exceptional protein supplements readily available at local health food stores that offer the highest possible protein efficiency ratios (or PER) and at relatively inexpensive prices, especially when compared to expensive cuts of meat and fish. The bottom line is that obtaining good lean protein sources is easier today than it has ever been. So rest assured you'll be able to feed your muscles and body tissues everything they need without breaking your bank account to do it.

Protein Requirements

So how much protein does your body need at any given time? According to scientific research, the human body can only absorb 30 to 40 grams of protein at any given time. Hence our recommendation to eat 5 to 6 small meals daily as opposed to 2 or 3 large meals. It's much easier on the body's digestion, and it allows for much more of the protein you consume to be utilized in body maintenance and muscle building. Over consumption of protein, at any given time, will either be stored as body fat or excreted from the body, causing a strain on the digestive system, and neither one is healthy option. Ideally, eat 5 to 6 small meals daily as opposed to 2 or 3 large meals.

Carbohydrates

During the 1990s, nutritional scientists (funded by the food processors) told people to avoid protein and all forms of *fat*—even the essential fatty acids that are necessary for life and normal cell function not to mention the body's ability to synthesize hormones. As a result of following these so-called dietary experts, diabetes and obesity skyrocketed to epidemic proportions. So much so that today an uninformed public is frightened to eat carbohydrates. *But carbs are not to blame!* As usual, misinformation is.

Here's how it worked. During the '90s, while we were bombarded with constant messages on television and in the print media about the dangers of fat, we were simultaneously blitzed with messages from food manufacturers telling us to eat their low-fat cakes, brownies, and cookies. What they neglected to tell us was that these processed products

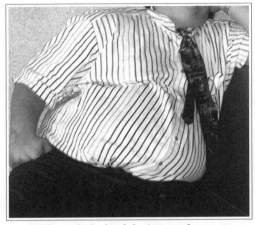

The end result of the '90s carb craze!

were super high in refined sugars and appetite-stimulating chemical additives that made people lose control over their appetites, thereby causing them to consume twice as many calories as they otherwise would have. To make matters worse, these products had almost no dietary fiber. America's consumption of these foods led to rampant obesity and diabetes nationwide. And what was blamed? You guessed it—carbohydrates.

Just as the right amount of proteins and fats is absolutely essential for health and overall well-being, so are carbohydrates. In fact, if you starve your body by not fueling it with the right kind of carbohydrates, you'll get to the point where you can't even think straight and you'll feel edgy all the time. But it's the right kind of carbohydrates that are essential to good health.

There are three types of carbohydrates: refined (manufactured by man); simple (natural occurring sugars created by God and found in an abundance of natural fruits); and complex (found in grains and vegetables of all types). Let's look at them individually.

Refined Carbohydrates

These are man-made sugars. Remember when I previously referred to that 20-ounce bottle of Coke? On the label it stated that it contained 250 calories and 60+ grams of sugar. No protein, no fat, no vitamins, no minerals (other than phosphoric acid which will destroy your skeletal tissues, muscles, bones, and connective tissue over time). Did I mention no fiber, but it does have caffeine and food coloring? That's it, folks. In other words, it has nothing but ultra-refined carbohydrates that require virtually no digestion, that go right into your bloodstream and cause an insulin spike, so that just as you feel a rush of energy, it's followed by an even bigger letdown. Then after these ultra-refined carbs have entered your bloodstream, where would you guess those 250 calories go if you don't burn them off in activity? Look down at your waist, because you'll be wearing them in body fat.

This is why refined sugars are so bad for you. They have been stripped of all life-giving nutrients, including vitamins, minerals, and dietary fiber. As a result, they can be immediately stored on the body. But also consider this: If sugar can be responsible for literally eating holes in tooth enamel, the hardest structure of your body, what else can it do? Bottom line: If you want to be strong and super healthy, it's essential to keep ultra-refined sugars (carbohydrates) to a minimum and consume them very infrequently. Does that mean never? Of course not. Even Charles Atlas said it was okay to eat sweets once in a while, provided that it was of the highest quality possible.

Simple Carbohydrates

These are the naturally occurring sugars found in an abundance of delicious fruits. The good news is that in the form provided by nature, you also get vitamins, minerals, water, and phytonutrients that are completely absent from processed, man-made refined sugars. So if you want to indulge in a dietary treat that's good for you, it's essential that you include an abundance of fresh fruits. Sweets as God intended.

Complex Carbohydrates

Complex carbohydrates come in the form of grains and vegetables. The molecular structure of these carbohydrates requires a gradual breakdown into glucose, which results in slowly released energy over a much larger period  of time (up to 4 hours) than simple carbohydrates or the refined, man-made version. For this reason vegetables (fresh, frozen, and canned) and whole grains should become your dietary mainstay with unprocessed simple carbohydrates (fruits) as your backup, and keep the ultra-refined carbohydrates as your binge-avoiding treat. Complex carbohydrates in their unrefined state give you plenty of dietary fiber and allow your appetite to feel satiated for longer periods of time. Yams, squash, potatoes, carrots, and virtually all whole grains, including rice, corn, oats, wheat, rye, and several others, offer incredible health benefits in helping to control cholesterol and improve your overall triglyceride profile.

Bottom line: Don't be afraid to eat unrefined carbohydrates as nature intended them. But do yourself a favor. Avoid all *refined* carbohydrates that are high in sugars and fats, such as pies, cookies, cakes, ice cream, potato chips, and all refined snack foods. These are the foods (if you want to call them that) that are responsible for both the obesity and diabetes epidemics in America today. The food processors would rather die than admit it, but that doesn't make it any less true.

Sodium—The Truth

Sodium, in combination with potassium, helps regulate body fluids and maintain the acid-alkali balance of the bloodstream. This sodium-potassium balance is necessary for many bodily functions, not the least of which is the ability of muscles to contract. This is why certain athletes develop cramps in the latter part of intense competitions when they have been sweating so much that this delicate balance becomes disrupted. Such episodes have cost many athletes world titles as happened to Muhammad Ali when he fought Leon Spinks the first time. He literally couldn't protect himself because he became so weak. In addition to losing the ability to control and contract muscles, insufficient sodium can also cause muscle shrinking and intestinal gas.

For this reason, it is not necessary for healthy people to completely eliminate sodium from their diet. And in any case, it would be very difficult to do because virtually everything we eat and drink contains some sodium. Tap water contains 10 milligrams of sodium in an 8-ounce glass. Club soda contains 25 milligrams per 8-ounce serving as do virtually all soft drinks. Even a slice of whole wheat bread contains 120 milligrams while a 6-ounce chicken breast contains 150 milligrams. So you see it really isn't difficult to obtain reasonable amounts of sodium.

So why is sodium considered to be so bad? Simple. Sodium holds up to 50 times its own weight in water. Excess sodium consumption results in water retention. In fact, it is not unusual for many people to carry 5 to 10 pounds of excess water in their bodies if they habitually consume extremely high sodium foods. This in turn can lead to problems such as high blood pressure.

Balance

Although Wendie and I do not believe it is necessary for a healthy person to totally deprive themselves of sodium, too much can cause all kinds of problems. So what we recommend is that you strive to stay between 1500 and 2500 milligrams daily. Foods that contain excessive amounts of sodium include all canned, smoked, and pickled foods, most frozen dinners, Chinese foods, pizza, frankfurters, and condiments such as table salt, ketchup, mustard, A-1 sauce, and Worcestershire sauce. These items can easily contain 1000 or more milligrams per serving, so go easy on these.

If you are one of the very few people who enjoys high sodium foods and has no problem with high blood pressure, and if you don't mind the temporary water weight gain obscuring the muscular definition of your abdominals and other muscle groups, it's probably not a big deal to indulge in pizza once in a while. All you need to do is to cut way back for a period of 3 to 5 days on sodium intake and drink lots of pure H_2O, and you'll eliminate any excess water and find that no real harm has been done.

Remember, water weight is not *real* weight. It's very temporary and can be flushed out of your system in a matter of days. Fat weight, on the other hand, is all *too real.* It sticks to your muscles and takes weeks to eliminate. But it too will go away.

Drink Lots of Water

Isn't it ironic that the best way to get rid of excess water weight is to drink more of it? It's true. The more water you drink, the less water you retain. You will also retain less water while eating high sodium foods if you drink a lot of water while eating. Drink a minimum of eight 12-ounce glasses of pure water daily. It's a great way to keep your skin looking younger and also gives your body a daily internal shower.

The Lean, Sculpted, Muscular Food Plan

Now that you know the basics about food, it's time to plan your new healthy eating style. The quintessence (I've always wanted to use that word) of the plan is simple. Wendie has compiled a Five Tier List of the best foods for getting lean, sculpted, and muscular on the hurry up. Starting with List One—"Best Foods to Get 'Ripped By' "—read all the way down through List Five—"Eat This Stuff Often and You'll Be Wearing It."

You'll have a complete and ready reference to review anytime and any-place. Best of all is the fact that if 80 percent of your food choices come from Lists One and Two, 15 percent come from List Three, and only 5 percent coming from Lists Four and Five, you will be awed by how easy it is to stay lean, hard, and sculpted. So here are the lists, the rest is up to you.

Good Luck!

FOOD LISTS	%
LISTS ONE & TWO	80%
LIST THREE	15%
LISTS FOUR & FIVE	5%

MIRACLE SEVEN FOOD PLANNER
for the Lean, Sculpted, Muscular Look

LIST ONE
BEST FOODS TO GET "RIPPED BY"

- Artichokes
- Beans, all varieties
- Bee pollen, organic
- Beets
- Blackberries
- Blueberries
- Boysenberries
- Bran
- **BROCCOLI**
- Brussels sprouts
- Cabbage
- Cantaloupe
- Carrots
- Cauliflower
- Cereals, whole grain only
- Citrus, raw fruits & juices w/no sugar added
- Cranberry juice, all natural
- Currants
- Egg whites
- Fish, cold water varieties (salmon, mackerel, cod)
- Garlic, fresh
- Grapes and grape juice, no added sugar
- Kale
- **KIWI FRUIT**
- Mangoes

- Milk, nonfat
- Mushrooms (portabello, miiake, and shitake)
- Nectarines
- Oatmeal, steel cut
- Olives
- Olive oil
- Onions
- **PAPAYAS**
- Peas
- Peppers, red and green
- Plums
- Protein drinks, whey protein low fat/low sugar
- Prunes
- Rice, brown
- Salsa
- Spinach, fresh
- Sweet potatoes
- Tea, green and black
- Tofu
- Tomatoes and tomato products
- Vegetable juices, fresh squeezed
- Water

EXCEPTIONAL FOODS FOR HEALTH & STRENGTH

- Almonds, raw
- Apples
- Asparagus
- **BANANAS**
- Barley
- Boca burgers
- Bread, sprouted whole grain
- Broccoli sprouts
- Buffalo steaks (lower in fat than chicken)
- Celery
- Cereal, dry, high-fiber varieties
- Cherries, fresh, all varieties
- Chicken, free range, skinless white meat
- Coffee, black
- Cottage cheese, low fat
- **CORN ON THE COB**
- Cucumbers
- Eggplant
- Goat's milk
- Fish, fresh water varieties
- Graham crackers
- Lettuce, romaine, leafy green, or red
- Lima beans
- Melon, honeydew
- Mushrooms (morels)
- Ostrich
- Pancakes, buckwheat

- Pasta, high protein, with marinara sauce, fish, or vegetables
- Peaches
- Pears
- Pecans
- **PINEAPPLE**
- Raisins
- Raspberries
- Rhubarb
- Ricotta cheese
- Shellfish, boiled or broiled
- Soy beans, edemame
- Soy milk
- Squash, butternut and summer
- Strawberries
- String beans
- Sunflower seeds
- Tuna, albacore packed in spring water
- Turkey breast
- Vegetable juice, canned or bottled
- Veggie burgers
- Walnuts

- **WATERMELON**
- Wine, red
- Yogurt, low-fat varieties
- Zucchini

GREAT FOOD! BUT USE LISTS ONE & TWO FOR RAPID FAT LOSS

- Applesauce
- Apricots
- **AVOCADOS**
- Bagels, whole grain
- Beef, eye of round
- Beef, extra lean ground
- Beef, London broil
- Beef, top round
- Canola oil
- Chicken, broiled
- Chicken taco, baked
- Chicken wrap, white meat
- Chocolate, dark natural
- Eggs, whole
- English muffins, whole grain
- French fries, baked
- Fruit, dried
- Fruit juice, unsweetened
- Granola, natural low fat
- Iced coffee and tea drinks with nonfat milk
- Jams and marmalade, all-natural fruit
- **LAMB, ROAST LEG**

- Margarine, fat free
- Mustard
- Nuts (walnuts, macadamia, pistachios, hazelnuts, pine nuts)
- Olives
- Pancakes
- Pasta, plain
- Peanut oil
- **PEANUTS**
- Peanut butter, all natural
- Pork tenderloin
- Potatoes, white
- Pretzels, whole grain
- Refried beans, low fat
- Rice cakes
- Rice, long grain basmati
- Sauerkraut
- Soups, canned broth
- Veal, roasted
- Wine, white
- Yogurt with natural fruit

BE CAREFUL! STILL, ONCE IN A WHILE IS NO BIG DEAL

- Beef (barbecued, filet mignon, rib eye, sirloin)
- **BEEF, LEAN GROUND**
- Beef stroganoff with fat-free sour cream
- Butter
- Caesar salad with chicken
- Canadian bacon
- Cheese, natural varieties only
- Chili
- Chinese food with lots of vegetables
- Chips, baked, low fat, whole grain
- **COFFEE CAKE**
- Crackers, whole grain
- Cream cheese, low fat
- Duck, roasted
- Energy bars, whole grain
- Fruits, canned in natural juices
- Grilled cheese sandwich, natural cheeses only
- Ham, ultra lean
- Honey
- Hot dogs, low fat
- Lettuce, iceberg
- Juices, sweetened w/pear juice
- Lamb chops
- Lasagna, low-fat meat or vegetable
- Lunch meat, deli style lean
- Macaroni and cheese

- Macaroni salad
- Mayonnaise, low fat
- Meat loaf
- Mexican food, not fried
- Milk, 2% butterfat
- Muffins
- Nut butters (almond/cashew)
- Peppers, stuffed
- **PIZZA**
- Popcorn w/butter
- Pork chops, ultra lean
- Potato salad
- Pudding, low fat
- Reuben sandwich or wrap
- Salads (chef's, chicken, cobb, tuna)
- Sherbet
- Sloppy Joe, ultra lean
- Sorbet made from fresh fruit
- Soups, creamed varieties
- Soy sauce
- Spaghetti with meatballs
- Submarine sandwich, ultra lean, low fat
- Taco salad, chicken or lean beef
- Turkey, ground
- Vegetable oils, cold processed

EAT THIS STUFF OFTEN AND YOU'LL BE WEARING IT!

- Bacon
- Beef, ground, regular
- Beef tacos, deep fried
- Breakfast sandwiches, fast food varieties
- **CAKES**
- Candies
- Cereals, pre-sugared
- Charred or blackened beef, chicken, or fish
- Cheese curds, deep fried
- Chicken divan
- Chicken nuggets
- Chicken wings, buffalo or sweet and sour
- Chicken sandwich, fried
- Chips, potato or corn, industrial strength regular
- Cinnamon buns, glazed
- Clams
- Clam chowder
- **COOKIES**
- Corn dogs
- Crab
- Cream cheese
- Creamed vegetables
- Creamer, nondairy
- Doughnuts, all varieties
- French fries

- Gravies
- Hamburger, fast food
- Hot dogs
- Ice cream, full-fat varieties
- Latte with whole milk
- Lobster Newburg
- Lunchmeat
- Mayonnaise, industrial strength
- Milk, whole
- Nacho chips with cheese
- Onion rings
- Pastries
- **PIES**
- Potatoes, fried
- Potato skins with standard toppings
- Pot pies
- Refried beans, the real ones in lard
- Salad dressings, full-fat varieties
- Sausages
- Shrimp, breaded and fried
- Soft drinks
- Spare ribs
- Tater tots
- Toaster pastries

There you have it. Follow this five tier list and it will be easy to stay in lean, well-muscled condition 24/7.

If you mess up once in a while, no big deal. Just concentrate on lists one, two, and three until you're back to lean.

Now let's look at some serious body sculpting from neck to toes!

The Miracle**SEVEN**

*Workout***ONE**

Chest

Shoulders

Triceps

UPPER BODY FOUNDATION—
CHEST, SHOULDERS, AND TRICEPS

I began training at the age of ten when my grandfather and Uncle Wally put me on the world famous "Charles Atlas Dynamic Tension Training System." For me it was literally a godsend. If you're familiar with the system, you know that the transformation of the chest, shoulders, and triceps was Lesson One of 12 weekly mail-order lessons Charles Atlas had students begin to work on—just as you will begin with here.

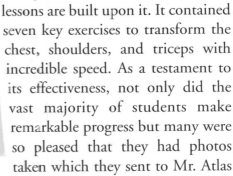

There are several reasons why Atlas made the upper body formation his first and foundational workout, but the primary reason is that his other eleven

lessons are built upon it. It contained seven key exercises to transform the chest, shoulders, and triceps with incredible speed. As a testament to its effectiveness, not only did the vast majority of students make remarkable progress but many were so pleased that they had photos taken which they sent to Mr. Atlas after just the first week.

Keep in mind that if Mr. Atlas was going to keep his students sending in their weekly money orders in the 1920s, it was paramount that they achieve incredible, immediate, and very gratifying results almost from day one. The fact that so few students ever dropped out tells you how fantastic the results really were. With that in mind, I want you to rest assured that the seven exercises you will be following will give you both immediate and sensational results that will be noticed almost from the get go.

In fact, these are the same exercises that Wendie began using just as soon as her shoulder healed as a result of her daily practice of The Tiger Moves. She said to me, "John, I want to be able to do two things I've never been able to do—pull-ups and handstand push-ups." Wendie would tell you what I've often heard her tell others, "These exercises began to work immediately." And, yes, Wendie can now do pull-ups and handstand push-ups.

The bottom line is that these exercises are just as beneficial for women as they are for men. In both cases the body starts to take on the lithe, highly defined, beautifully sculpted contours of a well-trained gymnast or martial artist. Following these exercises you can literally develop your body to its peak of natural perfection without ever worrying about becoming massively overdeveloped, yet your strength-to-body weight ratio will soar.

As Uncle Wally used to say, "You're gonna look like a perfectly developed athlete instead of like somebody who's been beaten on with a baseball bat to induce swelling."

That said, here are the seven exercises for chest, shoulder, and tricep transformation.

#1—PANTHER STRETCH PUSH-UP
#2—ATLAS PUSH-UP
#3—THE CAT
#4—LIEDERMAN CHEST PRESS
#5—C'MON AT YA!
#6—ROPE PULL DOWN
#7—PECTORAL PUSH DOWN WHILE SEATED

TRAINING NOTES

In the pages that follow, each exercise is shown individually with a complete written description.

At first try for 3 sets of 10 repetitions of each exercise. If you can't do that many, it's no big deal. Just do as many as you can. On the other hand, if you can do more, that's great. Charles Atlas told his students they should work up to performing 100 Atlas Push-ups each day and to divide the exercises (all seven) into morning and evening sessions. That way they were training twice daily. He also said that if "you are keen on developing a very big and powerful chest to aim for 200 repetitions each day of the Atlas Push-up." Break it up into 100 repetitions in the morning session and 100 repetitions in the evening.

That said, let's go!

PANTHER STRETCH PUSH-UP

Ready

Photo 1 shows perfect form for this exercise. Arms back and legs straight (an inverted "V"), looking directly at your feet.

Set

With arms remaining straight, lower your entire body from shoulders to feet, bending until your hips almost, but not quite, touch the floor.

Go

Return to start by retracing the exact movements in reverse. Arms remain straight throughout the movement.

TRAINING MEMO: *Men & Women*

At the beginning, anywhere from 15 to 25 repetitions is excellent. Once you can routinely do sets of 25 to 50, you will have superb shoulder, chest, arm, and both upper and lower back development.

PUSH-UPS BETWEEN CHAIRS
"ATLAS PUSH-UPS"

Ready

Feet on floor, hands placed on two chair seats a comfortable distance apart. The entire body is one straight line between heels and head looking straight ahead.

Set

Powerfully flex (contract) every muscle from arms to toes. Absolutely no sagging.

Go

Slowly descend into a push-up between chairs while maintaining tension in all moving muscles of the arms and chest. Without resting at the bottom, slowly push back to the straight arms position for one complete repetition. Continue until you have completed your entire set of 10 repetitions. Rest and continue for 2 more complete sets of 10 repetitions each. Then move immediately to the next exercise.

TRAINING MEMO: *Men & Women*

Maintaining tension and powerfully contracting each muscle as your body moves through this exercise dramatically lessens the number of repetitions you will be capable of completing. The key to this and all exercises is to think into and powerfully contract the muscles you are working—in this case, it is the pectorals of the chest.

"I have been caught practicing these push-ups on numerous occasions at the office. I enjoy being able to get a deep stretch while performing the Atlas Push-ups and have noticed a difference in my overall strength thanks to the variation options." – W.P.

Both strong women and men can perform this variation of the Atlas Push-up—Atlas II. The higher the feet are elevated the more difficult the exercise becomes.

REMEMBER: Keep the muscles of your abs and lower back contracted, absolutely no sagging.

"This was the first and most important exercise in the world famous Charles Atlas Dynamic Tension Bodybuilding course. It still works wonders today." – J.P.

CHEST, ABDOMINALS, AND TRICEPS DVR CONTRACTION
"THE C.A.T."

Ready

Stand straight with your feet at shoulder-width apart, hands shoulder level, fists pointed down with elbows lower than fists.

Set

Flex your arms, pecs, and abs powerfully.

Go

Against high tension generated by consciously contracting biceps, push down with great tension while maintaining tension in pecs, abs, and especially the triceps on the back of the upper arms.

TRAINING MEMO: *Men & Women*

Practice in front of a mirror and you will see the wide range of muscles that are exercised.

THE C.A.T. is one of the best upper body exercises in existence. It builds an all-around sculpted upper body.

SELF-RESISTANCE PECTORAL CONTRACTION
"LIEDERMAN CHEST PRESS"

Ready

Stand upright. Clasp hands in front of chest as shown in photo.

Set

Keeping your hands level in front of your chest, push one hand with the other and slowly build pressure until you are performing a maximum Isometric contraction. At that point ease off enough so you can begin to move while maintaining tension (your elbows will be lower than your hands).

Go

Using Dynamic Self-Resistance (DSR), slowly push back and forth across your chest as far as you can while maintaining tension. The harder you resist, the slower the movement. Earle Liederman said of this exercise, "This exercise will outline your pectoral muscles better than any other movement, as it hits them direct."

TRAINING MEMO: *Men & Women*

In time you will be able to use maximum contraction. At that point you will perform 3 to 5 repetitions for a maximum of 2 sets. To start, though, just use moderate tension for 3 sets of 10 repetitions. And remember, ladies, it will work as well for you as it does for the guys.

LIEDERMAN CHEST PRESS sculpts pecs, arms, and shoulders equally well for men and women.

C'MON AT YA!

Ready

With hands in a prayer posture close to the chest (you may want to thank God that the first four exercises are over) apply intense pressure from both hands. You'll feel it on the inner side of both pectorals.

Set

While maintaining the pressure, slowly begin to extend both hands straight out.

Go

Once you reach full extension, slowly reverse direction and bring both hands back to the chest while maintaining tension in arms, pectorals, shoulders, upper back, and abs.

TRAINING MEMO: *Men & Women*

This exercise is especially good for outlining the inner portion of the pectoral muscles, but also exercises the entire upper body.

ROPE PULL DOWN

Ready

Begin with your hands one on top of the other in fists as though placed around an imaginary rope. Start pulling down with your top fist while your bottom fist is resisting powerfully.

Set

While maintaining tension, lower the tension in your bottom fist just enough to allow your top fist to pull down.

Go

Continue pulling to your waistline, then reverse the direction of your hand resisting while your bottom hand moves back to the top position.

TRAINING MEMO: *Men & Women*

Once you get "the hang" of this movement, you will be awed by the "double action duty" of this one exercise. It is a powerful exercise for the entire upper body.

PECTORAL PUSH DOWN
WHILE SEATED

Ready

Start in the extended position shown and powerfully contract your arms, shoulders, pecs, abs, and quadriceps (don't worry, it's automatic).

Set

Slowly lower as far as you can comfortably while maintaining tension in all the muscle groups described.

Go

After you reach the lowest position, hold for "one tiger one," then push back slowly to the starting position.

TRAINING MEMO: *Men & Women*

You can also do a less advanced phase of this exercise while sitting in a chair without armrests. Grasp the seat with both hands and raise your body slightly with your legs extended.

The Miracle SEVEN

Workout TWO

Powerful Arms

V-Shaped Back

Muscular Neck

POWERFUL ARMS, A V-SHAPED BACK,
AND A LITHE, MUSCULAR NECK

I'm often asked, especially by very young men, if it's really possible to build a beautiful, symmetrically developed physique without ever touching weights, going to a gym, or relying on machines. Naturally, I emphatically make the case that not only is it possible, but for lifelong strength and pain-free vigor it's far and away *the best way*. After all, that's exactly what I've done.

But to make my case rock solid, I'd like to introduce you to Gordon Anderson, a special friend of mine who has made incredible contributions to the world of physical culture. Gordon's fascination with strength and physical culture dates back to when he was a little boy looking at the Charles Atlas ads featured so prominently on the back covers of comic books during the 1950s. Just as I did, Gordon became a Charles Atlas student and achieved superior results.

In early October 1962, Gordon was doing his stint at The U.S. Army Infantry School in Fort Benning, Georgia. For an Atlas student in Gordon's shape, the training was a breeze and he was having a great time...*until* October 21 when the Cuban Missile Crisis got underway. With the United States and the Soviet Union literally on the brink of nuclear war, Gordon was transitioned into training with the Army Rangers. Because of the imminent threat of all-out war with the Soviets, the Rangers put the guys from the Infantry School through the most physically and psychologically demanding training imaginable. Although Gordon was in excellent shape, the Rangers purposed to push every candidate to the very edge of his capabilities, which meant far beyond what any normal person would consider their limits.

Gordon said to me about his training, "John, I never wanted to do another push-up again as long as I lived." But push-ups he did, and push-ups he does to this day. Now, more than 40 years later and in his mid 60s, Gordon can still kick some serious butt as well as do sets of 100 consecutive push-ups anytime he feels like it. Bottom line: Gordon Anderson represents what lifelong fitness and functional strength is all about. After all, less than 5 percent of all 20 years olds can do 100 consecutive push-ups in good form. When it comes to 60 year olds…well, you get my point.

Gordon Anderson is a fantastic resource when it comes to building powerful biceps, a V-shaped back, and a neck that is a pillar of strength. He has collected the finest physical culture courses from the late 1880s and forward and has worked with his friends Gilbert Waldron and Roger Fillary in creating one of the most comprehensive web sites on the entire worldwide web, "Sandow & the Golden Age of Iron Men." Just type that into your browser and you should have no problem finding it. Once there, you can go through scores of the most incredible physical culture courses ever written and created. And get this—*it's free of charge.* No, I'm not joking. At $100 a year, it would be a bargain, but Gordon, Gil, and Roger have made it available to one and all free of charge. I, for one, am very grateful. Thanks, guys!

If you go to their web site, I want you to click on the "Atlas" box that's in the lower center of the screen. Entering this portion of the web site, you'll see articles by and about Charles Atlas, but I want you to pay special attention

Photos courtesy of Sandow & the Golden Age of Iron Men

to the Atlas promotional brochures that feature dozens of photos of Mr. Atlas's students. Take a look at the extraordinary arm, back, and neck development that virtually every student displays. Keep in mind that in most cases the photos were taken after just 12 weeks of Atlas Dynamic Tension Training. Amazed? You most certainly should be, especially because these men accomplished these superb Greek god type physiques without ever touching weights, machines, or even a chinning bar (chinning was not a part of the Atlas course).

So what did they do? They performed a series of Dynamic Self-Resistance (DSR) and Dynamic Visualized Resistance (DVR) exercises to achieve these great results. No weights, no gym, and no equipment of any kind. Consider how their patience, perseverance, and determination paid off!

In this workout, I'll supply the know-how with seven superb exercises to sculpt your back, biceps, and neck. You supply the patience, perseverance, and determination. You've already laid the foundation for superior development with The Tiger Moves and Workout #1 for your chest, shoulders, and triceps. Truth to tell, you've already been working your back intensively, so these exercises provide the finishing touches. Now let's go.

HOLD ON, HERE BOYS. I have a special word for the ladies *only*. So, guys, if you aren't wearing a bra, then get lost.

Ladies, you're aware of the trouble spot—the areas on your back above and below your bra straps that make it look like you're wearing your kid sister's bra. Everywhere you look, you'll see women who are losing their battle with the bra straps. One way to make this fatty area less noticeable is to go braless, but that creates an even more noticeable set of problems. Besides, the "flower power" days have passed, and it's been a long time since women burned bras.

So, what's the solution? It's a healthy, realistic solution—diet and exercise. Diet and nutrition were detailed in Chapter 7. In this workout, we focus on Transformetric exercises that quickly slim away all those extra rolls you hate, and they'll sculpt your back, leaving it strong, smooth, and shapely.

Most of us get dressed in front of a two-way mirror. We might change our perception of our body image if we went to a three-way mirror. We tend to forget about what we can't see—"out of sight, out of mind," so to speak. But to ignore the overall appearance of your physique is comparable to styling only the front part of your hair. How silly is that? From your head to your heels, the rear view is as important as the front. Unsightly back fat is unappealing to the eye, and it's bad for your health. People with large deposits of back fat almost always experience back pain.

If you've ever experienced a painful back, you realize that your back is involved in almost every move you make throughout the day. It's all too easy to take a healthy back for granted. Whether it's upper or lower back pain, four out of five adults have the "Oh, My Aching Back" syndrome at least once during their life. For people under the age of 45, back pain is the most common cause of disability. How many people do you hear complain about their backs?

I used to work out with a personal trainer, lift weights, go to body pump classes, and lift my son repeatedly throughout the day (incorrectly, by the way). I got to the point where the pain was so intense in my lower back that I had to lie on my back with my knees bent and propped up just to fall asleep. If I didn't start out in this position, the agonizing pain would keep me up all night counting sheep.

It amazes me just how much everyday life can put the wear and tear on our backs. But if you add weightlifting as I did, or if you're carrying excess pounds of fat that crank up the scale, your joints, tendons, and ligaments will pay the price. Extra weight compresses the spine, and eventually your body will send the painful signal that you have a problem.

Even though you can't turn back time, you can recover from most back injuries or pain. Chiropractic clinics across the country are selling our books because Transformetrics™ aids the healing of their patients. According to a study from the Mayo Clinic, strong back muscles help "prevent the disfiguring effect of osteoporosis on spinal posture and reduce the risk of vertebral compression fractures," and

that's what Transformetrics™ can do for you…and more.

After reaching my goal through Transformetrics™ to do handstand push-ups and pull-ups without assistance, I started noticing the definition of my "lats" for the first time. Initially, I wasn't 100 percent sure that I liked them, but then I started getting compliments. One of the bonus features of creating a strong lean back is that the "V" appearance actually makes your waistline look smaller! And I felt stronger, healthier, and *my back was wonderfully pain-free.* How delightful to no longer suffer from sleepless nights and achy days!

So let's get to the exercises that vanquish unsightly bra fat as well as strengthen and sculpt your back to leave you pain-free for life!

#1—NECK FLEX
#2—ATLAS LAT PULL
#3—BACK FLEX
#4—REVERSE BACK FLEX
#5—DYNAMIC SELF-RESISTANCE CURLS
#6—SIDE ARM FLEX
#7—CONCENTRATION CURL

NECK FLEX

Ready

While standing or sitting, bend your head back as far as it will go. Place your hands on your forehead. Now bend your head forward smoothly as far as possible against dynamic self-resistance provided by your hands. Aim for 10 smooth repetitions.

Set

From the same position, bend your head forward as far as it will go. Place your hands behind your head as shown and against dynamic self-resistance bend your head up and back as smoothly as possible. Aim for 10 repetitions.

Go

From the same position with your face looking forward, bend your head down to the left as close to the shoulder as possible. Then place your right hand on the right side of your head just above the ear. Move your head smoothly to the upright position while providing dynamic self-resistance with your right hand. Aim for 10 repetitions.

Then reverse everything by bending your head to the right shoulder and placing the palm of your left hand just above the ear. Move your head to the upright position smoothly against the dynamic self-resistance of your left hand. Aim for 10 repetitions.

TRAINING MEMO: *Men & Women*

When you first start this exercise, go easy. Most people have never exercised their neck muscles. So don't overdo it.

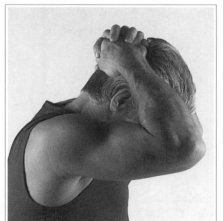
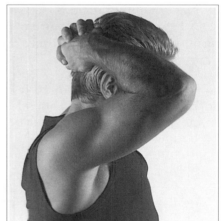

ATLAS LAT PULL

Ready
While standing with your feet shoulder-width apart, lean forward at the waist and interlock the fingers of both hands around the back of your left leg just above where it bends at the knee.

Set
Now smoothly stand back to the upright position as you slowly lift your leg with you. Resistance is provided by the leg muscles working against both arm and latissimus dorsi muscles.

Go
After completing up to 10 repetitions switch legs and complete up to 10 repetitions with the other leg. There is no need to ever go beyond 3 sets of 10. But use the chart below to determine both intensity and repetitions.

REPETITIONS		SETS
MODERATE	8-10	3 max
HEAVY	6-8	2-3 max
VERY HEAVY	3-5	2 max

TRAINING MEMO: *Men & Women*

This exercise is especially good for bringing out the latissimus dorsi muscles of the upper back. But it also works wonders for your biceps and lower back as well as your sense of balance.

BACK FLEX

Ready

Stand upright with your feet shoulder-width apart. Grasp your hands as shown behind your back at approximately waist high.

Set

Powerfully push your shoulders downward and backward and bend your head and back as far back as you can.

Go

Hold this position as you perform a Transformetric Flex and tense the muscles as hard as possible. Perform up to 7 to 10 flexes, holding each for 10 seconds at the peak of the contraction.

The difference between a Transformetric Flex and an Isometric Contraction is that with a Transformetric Flex we flex our muscles to the maximum and hold for up to 10 seconds. With an Isometric Contraction we contract against an opposing force or object that is immovable.

TRAINING MEMO: *Men & Women*

This exercise works all the muscles of the upper back, including the trapezius. Although it may feel awkward at first, this movement will start to feel very natural after a short period of time. You will be astounded and pleased at your results—a strong, powerful, muscular back.

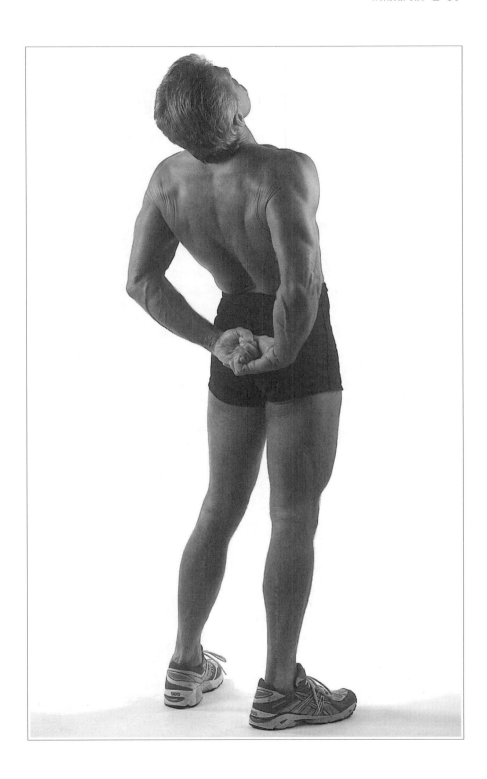

REVERSE BACK FLEX

Ready

Lie face down across a cushioned stool or chair with your hands clasped behind your head.

Set

Slowly and with great tension arch your entire back upward while simultaneously raising your head and feet upward. This is a very short but powerful movement.

Go

When your peak contraction is reached on your tenth repetition, try to flex and hold for a 10-second isometric contraction. At this point think into and powerfully contract your deltoid (shoulder) muscles. Do 3 sets maximum of this movement.

TRAINING MEMO: *Men & Women*

This is an extremely difficult and result-producing exercise. It is great for stretching and limbering up as well. Do it often.

DYNAMIC SELF-RESISTANCE CURLS

Ready

While standing or sitting, grasp your right wrist with your left hand. Your right hand is in a tight fist, palm up.

Set

Flex your wrist to engage the forearm muscles.

Go

As smoothly as possible bend your right arm at the elbow, pulling it up to the right shoulder while resisting the pull as your left hand pushes down powerfully. After completing 10 repetitions, switch arms and repeat with your left arm pulling up and your right arm pushing down.

TRAINING MEMO: *Men & Women*

This is an excellent exercise for building powerful biceps.

SIDE ARM FLEX

Ready

Place your right upper arm at your side and your forearm across your chest. Your left hand goes over the back of your right wrist.

Set

Against the powerful dynamic self-resistance provided by your left hand, slowly raise your right forearm outward and upward.

Go

Your right upper arm remains as close to your side as possible and does not rise at the shoulder. Perform up to 10 repetitions, then switch arms and continue for 10 more repetitions.

TRAINING MEMO: *Men & Women*

This exercise reaches the muscles on the side of the upper arm that routinely get missed in most workouts. The stronger the resistance that is supplied by the opposing hand, the fewer the repetitions that are required.

CONCENTRATION CURL

Ready

While sitting, position your right elbow on your right thigh and flex your muscles.

Set

Slowly curl your right fist to your right shoulder.

Go

Contract the biceps powerfully at the top of the movement. On the last repetition contract as powerfully as possible in Transformetric Flex for 10 seconds. Then switch arms and repeat with your left arm.

TRAINING MEMO: *Men & Women*

This is a phenomenal exercise for both the biceps and forearms.

The Miracle**SEVEN** *for women*

*Workout***THREE**

Quads

Glutes

Hips

Calves

QUADS, GLUTES, HIPS, AND CALVES—
ESPECIALLY FOR WOMEN

I f you were to take a survey and ask women what they feel is their main trouble zone, most would say their problem is the lower half of their bodies—the quads, glutes, hips, and calves. Having had my first child, I know the challenge well, which is the focus of this chapter. But men are not excluded from the battle (just look around and the facts speak for themselves). Banishing cellulite and creating strong lean muscles throughout the legs and glutes while slimming the hips is a goal for many. Matter of fact, John Peterson has been practicing my leg routine and experienced great results (even though I learned a couple of these exercises from him).

It's important for men and women alike to build and reshape their bodies evenly. If you train unevenly, you can end up looking inflated and puffed up like Mighty Mouse, which is an uneven, unappealing look. Believe me, you'll get noticed if you build up your upper body while not shaping your lower body accordingly, but you won't be able to control the snickering behind your back.

So how do we build and reshape our bodies evenly? Some gimmicky ads tell you all you need to do is use leg shaping gel, restorative leg cream, or even slim down mousse to get toned limbs without the sweat. One ad insists that their denier stretch lycra stockings include special time-released microcapsules filled with natural ingredients to smoothe, firm, and reduce cellulite—not to mention, you will soon see a reduction in your thigh size "in ONLY 21 days!" My favorite ad is for a product that "is proven" to reduce your dress size and cellulite with just a small clinical patch that delivers natural botanicals to stimulate your metabolism. And then there is an actress famous for a 1970s sitcom who advertises the "Thigh Master" and has been shown in magazines leaving a liposuction clinic. If you believe the ads in the media today, call me. I have a bridge for sale.

Over the years people have watched mainstream sports and selected the physiques of athletes whose strong, sleek, and overall desirable look is one they wish to mimic and hopefully obtain. When it comes to legs, the best legs belong to dancers, gymnasts, and those involved with martial arts. Although not everyone considers these athletes as the leaders in the leg development department, their amazing strength is all natural and comes from body weight training alone, and the look is aesthetically pleasing to the eye. This is the look that Transformetrics™ brings.

Other athletes typically practice with weights, which gives a completely different look—a bulky, exaggerated look. And the constant use of weights opens the door to the risk of injury to the joints, tendons, and ligaments. Think about how many people you know who have had some type of reconstructive knee surgery. Over time the tendons, joints, and ligaments end up literally being compressed, stretched, and pulled in ways that God never designed for them. When using Transformetrics™, this is never an issue.

Whether this is your first or final attempt at losing body fat and inches around your lower region, you will find your frustrations disappear in their tracks and you will never have to hide behind baggy or loose clothing again. (Which, oddly enough, makes you look that much heavier than you really are. Granted, I'm not telling you to bring out your "Daisy Duke" shorts or anything, but just don't exaggerate your shape with baggy outfits.) Transformetrics™ will reshape you in a way where the word *insecurity* will no longer exist in your vocabulary!

So wait no longer. These exercises will shrink your legs, glutes, and hips and allow for those jeans you've had buried in your closest for years to come out and be worn again. No more jumping up and down, trying to squeeze into your favorite jeans, or lying on the bed trying to zip them up with a coat hanger (yes, there was a time when

I used to wear jeans this tight). Skin tight may not be the style of the moment, thank goodness, but give it a few years and it will be back, and we better be ready!

That said, here are the seven exercises to create the shapely, strong legs of a dancer.

#1—FUREY SQUAT
#2—WALL SQUAT AND HOLD
#3—REVERSE LUNGE WITH LEG EXTENSION
#4—BALANCE SQUAT WITH C'MON AT YA!
#5—SIDE HINGE WITH BACK EXTENSION
#6—SISSY SQUAT
#7—HAMSTRING PRESS OUT

TRAINING NOTES

In the pages that follow, each exercise is shown individually with a complete written description.

At first try for 3 sets of 10 repetitions of each exercise with the exception of the "Wall Squat and Hold." If you can't do that many, it's no big deal. Just do as many as you can. On the other hand, if you can do more, that's great.

FUREY SQUATS

Ready

Feet approximately shoulder-width apart. Toes straight ahead. Hands in tight fists at shoulder level. Inhale deeply.

Set

While keeping your back relatively straight (don't bend forward), bend your knees and descend to the bottom position. Note the position of the hands reaching behind your back during the descent and brushing your knuckles on the ground at the bottom.

Go

When you arrive at the bottom position, you will rise naturally to your toes. At this point your arms continue swinging forward and upward while simultaneously pushing off your toes and rising to the original standing position. Your hands now form tight fists close to your sides at chest level. Inhale as you pull them in, exhale as you lower your body.

Repeat as smoothly and steadily as you can. Once you begin you'll notice that the arms take on a smooth, rhythmic motion similar to rowing a boat.

TRAINING MEMO: *Men & Women*

Okay, I learned this one from John, and I made this a part of my overall routine. The entire movement is done in one continuous, smooth movement. Sets of 10 to 15 are a great start. This is superb for your balance and calves.

WALL SQUAT AND HOLD

Ready

Start with your feet approximately 20" from the wall.

Set

Slowly lower your body into a parallel squat. Your back should be touching the wall.

Go

Hold this position as long as you can—up to 3 minutes. Yes, the muscles will begin to shake.

This form of exercise is called a Transformetric Hold. It is very similar to an Isometric Contraction but rather than contracting against an immovable object or force, we use muscle contraction alone to maintain the position.

TRAINING MEMO: *Men & Women*

It's best to only perform this exercise up to three times a week as it puts stress on the nervous system (but in a good way!). Hint: Read while in this position, and the time will fly!

REVERSE LUNGE W/LEG EXTENSION

Ready

Step back with your right leg into a lunge position, keeping your torso erect.

Set

Make sure to keep your left knee in line with your heel and not over your toes (at a 90° angle).

Go

Using your glutes and quad muscles, straighten your left leg and bring your right knee to just below hip height. Without leaning back, use your quad muscles to straighten your leg. Hold for 5 counts before returning to the starting position. Repeat, then switch legs.

TRAINING MEMO: *Men & Women*

Avoid locking either knee when doing this exercise. Doing so creates hyper extension and can wear out joint tissue over time.

BALANCE SQUAT W/C'MON AT YA!

Ready

Stand with your feet slightly wider than shoulder-width apart, toes turned out, and hands in prayer position.

Set

Pull your navel into your spine. You are now in the correct position for this exercise.

Go

Keeping your back straight, bend your knees into a squat until your thighs are almost parallel to the ground. Arch up high on your toes to strengthen your calves as well as practice balance. At the same time, perform the C'mon at Ya! from Workout One – Exercise #5. This combination provides you with one of the best full body exercises you could possibly do.

TRAINING MEMO: *Men & Women*

It helps to keep your balance if you focus on a certain object or spot in front of you.

SIDE HINGE W/BACK EXTENSION

Ready

Get a chair or something sturdy to hold on to that is waist high.

Set

Hold on to the chair to prepare for hinge.

Go

Lift your left leg in a side hinge position. Then, while still contracting, push your leg through until the leg is fully extended. Repeat 10 times, then reverse using the right leg.

TRAINING MEMO: *Men & Women*

Try not to lean forward when performing this exercise.

SISSY SQUAT

Ready

Set your feet about 12" apart and hands outstretched or on your hips to keep your balance.

Set

Select a focal point on a wall or other object to help maintain your balance.

Go

Slowly lower your body by squatting down. Maintain the position (hips forward) throughout the exercise. Raise and lower slowly. 12 to 20 reps is ideal.

TRAINING MEMO: *Men & Women*

Awesome for quads and glutes! Most effective if performed up on toes.

HAMSTRING PRESS OUT

Ready

Start with your legs together.

Set

Visualize that there is a wall behind you that you are pressing against for optimal tension.

Go

Raise your left leg while fully contracting your hamstring. Now press out while contracting your hamstring and glute muscles. Return your extended leg to the other leg, then back to the starting position. Reverse with the other leg.

TRAINING MEMO: *Men & Women*

Avoid locking your supporting knee.

The Miracle**SEVEN**

*Workout***FOUR**

Sculpted Abs

Core Strength

THE CORE OF STRENGTH—SCULPTED ABS
AND STRENGTH TO THE CORE

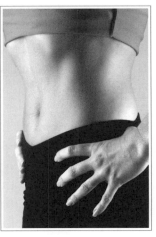

The way things are going these days I'm convinced it won't be long before television producers add a whole new category to the annual Emmy Awards. The category will be: Best Ab Infomercial.

Seriously, unless you've lived in a cave for the last decade, you can see an ab infomercial anytime of the day or night. In fact, there is currently an "Ab Shocker" infomercial in which a member of Britain's Royal Family smiles and confidently struts forward as she says she shocked herself lean. (You know, that belt device with the electrodes that shock your abs and cause them to contract involuntarily because it is assumed that the user is too lazy to contract his or her own abdominals.) Does it surprise you that this attractive lady does not give one word of credit to the Beverly Hills physicians who performed her extensive liposuction or even to Weight Watchers, whom she used to endorse? (So much for gratitude and long-term contracts.) No, according to her, it's the Ab Shocker that made her lean.

Then there is the commercial featuring the sincere, handsome young doctor—the one who looks so sincere you'd think he's a TV evangelist. In his first commercial he said, "If you have only 5 to 10 pounds to lose, this product is not for you." Can you imagine how many bottles of that stuff were sold when he said that? Or how about his follow-up commercial where he smiles and says, "It's not your fault that you're fat.... It's because your body is releasing too much of the stress hormone cortisol." Think about that statement, then read on.

By implication both the "Ab Shocker" and the cortisol blocking pills sold by the handsome young doctor who wouldn't kid you about anything are playing to the old "something for nothing" routine that is aimed directly at the gullible. Believe me, I'm being kind. P. T. Barnum would have just said, "There's a sucker born every minute."

But it makes me wonder what will be said next. Maybe something along this line: "It's not your fault, and it has nothing to do with those super-sized fries you eat every day or those double quarter pound cheeseburgers or even all those Krispy Kreme Donuts you down every day. No, it's because your body is overstressed and releasing too much of the cortisol hormone." My response to that is, "Yeah, right, your body is overstressed because you've been feeding it nothing but junk all day."

Think about it. The only way you can create lean, well-muscled abs is by following a combination of an ultra-lean nutritious diet that fuels you maximally with great tasting, health-building food (like the one you've already read about in this book) and a program of body friendly, ab-sculpting, fat-burning exercise that speeds your metabolism as you build lithe, strong, beautifully sculpted abdominal muscles.

So what is this magical program you'll be reading about here? Well, first off, get rid of the word *magic*. There is no abracadabra involved. But I do want you to do one thing before we go any further. Back in Workout #2 I told you about my friend Gordon Anderson and his

many contributions to the "Sandow & the Golden Age of Iron Men" web site, which is literally a museum of physical culture history (www.sandowplus.co.uk). I encouraged you to go there, scroll down to the last entry, then enter the Charles Atlas section and review the promotional brochures that show the results that Atlas students achieved. I asked you to study the impressive arm (biceps) and back development these men achieved without ever touching a weight or a chinning bar. If you followed my advice, I know you were awed by what you saw.

Now I'm asking you to go back to those same promotional brochures and take special notice of the abdominal development of those same Atlas students. Once again, you'll be awed by their "Greek god" like symmetry and perfectly sculpted abs. I mention this because not one of these perfect specimens ever heard of an Ab Roller, Ab Shocker, Six Second Abs, or any  other device. No weights, no gym, and no equipment were necessary to achieve those superior results. They just used a diet similar to the one in this book and a series of special ab-sculpting exercises that had the "rectus abdominus" showing prominently in no time.

Bottom line: It worked like a dream for Atlas students back then, and it will work like a dream for you today.

Let's get to the seven ab-sculpting exercises that will have you ripped in no time:

#1—ATLAS SIT-UPS
#2—ATLAS LEG RAISE
#3—V SIT-UPS
#4—ATLAS COMBINATION CRUNCH
#5—REVERSE CRUNCH
#6—KNEE PULL-IN
#7—OBLIQUE CRUNCH

FULL RANGE ATLAS SIT-UPS

Ready

Lie on the floor with your hands behind your head.

Set

With legs straight, imagine trying to force your heels into the floor. Tuck your chin toward your chest to contract your abs.

Go

Now slowly raise your upper body and bend forward as far as is comfortable. Charles Atlas wanted you to touch your forehead to your knees, but go only a far as you are comfortable and then slowly return to starting position for one repetition.

TRAINING MEMO: *Men & Women*

The secret to the effectiveness of this exercise is that the feet are not held down by anything other than muscular contraction. If your feet are held down, it ruins the exercise. Atlas recommended up to 100 reps daily done in 4 or 5 sets or all at once. It's your choice.

"Yes, it's as good for women as it is for men." – W.P.

FULL RANGE ATLAS LEG RAISE

Ready

Lie on the floor with your hands lightly cradling your buttocks.

Set

Begin by flexing the abdominal muscles and thinking into this muscle group as…

Go

You raise both legs together as far as possible, pelvis curls up and forward, and continue as far as is comfortable. Then slowly return to start position.

Start with 3 sets of however many you can comfortably do. Advanced Atlas students worked up to 100 either in sets or performed all at once.

TRAINING MEMO: *Men & Women*

Charles Atlas wanted his students to get to the point where they could touch the floor above their head with their toes. But go only as far as you are comfortable. The requisite flexibility will come about naturally. You must not try to force it. Doing so could pull or even tear muscles, so never push yourself to the edge of pain.

FULL RANGE ATLAS LEG RAISE is equally beneficial for men and women.

V SIT-UPS

Ready

Arms extended straight over your head. Toes pointed. Abdominals contracted.

Set

While thinking into your abs, begin to slowly and simultaneously raise your upper and lower body to the position shown.

Go

Endeavor to touch your toes and then slowly reverse direction while under complete control and return to the starting position for one repetition.

Start with 3 sets of as many as are comfortable and work up to a goal of 4 sets of 25.

TRAINING MEMO: *Men & Women*

Maintain a slow concentrated motion in both directions while keeping the muscles contracted powerfully. This is an excellent exercise for both men and women.

ATLAS COMBINATION SIT-UP/KNEE-UP

Ready

Lie on floor with your hands behind your head and your legs straight.

Set

Begin by raising your feet about 6" from the floor and flexing your abdominal muscles.

Go

Simultaneously sit up while bringing your knees toward your chest or even to chin level. At the top of the movement powerfully contract for "one tiger one." Slowly reverse direction and lower to floor for one repetition.

Start with 3 sets of whatever is comfortable and work up to 4 sets of 25 repetitions.

TRAINING MEMO: *Men & Women*

It takes a while to coordinate this movement. But it's a great exercise and was featured in *Physical Culture Magazine* of 1938 as one of Charles Atlas's favorite exercises. Slow, steady movement is the key.

THE ATLAS COMBINATION not only sculpts beautiful abs but also enhances balance and coordination.

REVERSE CRUNCH

Ready

Lie flat on your back with your head raised and arms and legs positioned as shown.

Set

Simultaneously raise your shoulders and knees, holding the peak contraction for "one tiger one, one tiger two."

Go

Return to the original position while maintaining the tension.

Begin with 3 sets of as many as are comfortable and work up to 4 sets of 25 repetitions.

TRAINING MEMO: *Men & Women*

Reverse crunches are an excellent way to work your lower abs. Keep your abs tight during the entire movement of this exercise.

KNEE PULL-IN

Ready

Position yourself in a chair as shown.

Set

Slowly raise your legs as high as possible. As you reach the peak of the movement, tighten your abs the best you can and hold for a count of "one tiger one, one tiger two."

Go

Slowly lower your legs…very slowly.

Start with 3 sets and work up to 4 sets of 25 repetitions.

TRAINING MEMO: *Men & Women*

Are you surprised by the intensity of this exercise? It's one you can do just about anywhere, anytime.

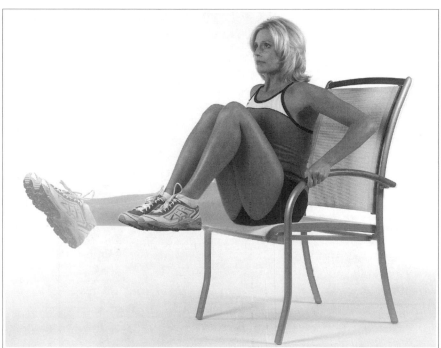

OBLIQUE CRUNCH

Ready

Lie down on your side and position your legs and arms as shown.

Set

The obliques are worked by bending your knees and raising and lowering the upper body in a controlled turn at the waist.

Go

Slowly return to the original position.

Once again, start with 3 sets and gradually work up to 4 sets of 25 repetitions.

TRAINING MEMO: *Men & Women*

A partner may be used to help keep your knees down. Perform an equal number of repetitions on both sides of the body.

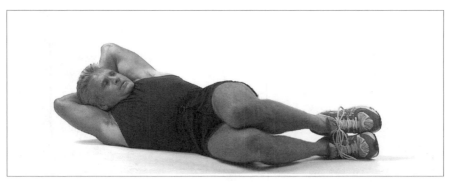

The Miracle SEVEN

Workout FIVE

Awesome Arms

V-Shaped Back

Pillar of Strength

The Miracle SEVEN WORKOUT 5

AWESOME ARMS, A V-SHAPED BACK, AND A PILLAR OF STRENGTH

In Workout #2, Wendie and I gave you seven foundational exercises to rapidly build, shape, and strengthen the muscles of your neck, back, and arms. If followed faithfully, these seven exercises will produce powerfully developed biceps and forearms, a strong, beautifully muscled back, and a slim, athletic looking neck that projects both youthfulness and vitality. Today we're going to build on that foundation for those who want to reach the epitome of athletic strength and functional fitness in sport.

To accomplish this we will be utilizing seven key exercises. Whereas in Workout #2 we presented seven exercises that could be equally beneficial whether you were just starting out or were already very advanced, this time we're focusing on super advanced training only. To accomplish this I'm relying on a series of exercises I learned from two men whom I greatly admire and respect, my friends Matt Furey and Mark De Lisle.

The seven exercises are:

#1—THE FUREY BRIDGE
#2—BEHIND THE NECK PULL-UP
#3—STANDARD WIDE GRIP PULL-UP
#4—STANDARD MARINE PULL-UP
#5—CLOSE GRIP PULL-UP
#6—CLOSE GRIP CHIN-UP
#7—COMMANDO PULL-UP

All seven exercises are very advanced. Only strong, well-conditioned men and women should attempt this workout.

Although I personally practice the Furey Bridge as pictured for a minimum of 3 minutes each day, if you experience severe discomfort or pain you *must* substitute the neck resistance series from Workout #2.

The six pull-up and chin-up variations are the exact exercises used to bring Navy SEALs to the peak of foundational athletic strength and fitness. My friend Mark De Lisle, who was a Navy SEAL and is the author of the *Navy SEAL Breakthrough to Master Level Fitness*, has emphasized that the variations of these pull-ups and chin-ups will create the off-the-chart strength-to-body weight ratios that Navy SEALs are known for. And Mark should know. He was capable of climbing an anchor chain at close to light speed so a terrorist wouldn't be able to get a crosshair on him with a night vision scope.

THE MOST CONTROVERSIAL EXERCISE

Before you consider performing this exercise you must get clearance from your physician or chiropractor—otherwise forget it!

Matt Furey is world famous for his *Combat Conditioning Training System* of all-natural body weight exercises, which he learned from his mentor, Karl Gotch. Mr. Gotch told Matt that although *all* the exercises contained in the combat conditioning training system are excellent, there are three that are absolutely essential. These three are what Matt refers to as "The Royal Court." They include the Furey (Hindu) Push-up, the Furey (Hindu) Squat, and the Furey (Back) Bridge.

Of the three exercises, Mr. Gotch told Matt that the single most beneficial was the Back Bridge because it strengthens and stretches the entire body in a way that no other exercise could even remotely begin to duplicate. Frankly, at first I was very skeptical. But after working at it for several months in order to get my flexibility as well as my strength to the point where I could sustain a "Nose to the Mat Bridge" (as pictured) for 3 full minutes, I was sold. And as you can see in the photos, so is Wendie.

METHODS OF PROGRESSION

Pull-ups and chin-ups maximize your body's own natural weight resistance. For most people they are among the most difficult exercises to perform. Mastering them allows you to achieve a strength-to-body ratio that is truly extraordinary. This is why elite members of our nation's Special Forces place so much emphasis on this one exercise.

Progression is generally slower with this exercise than others because you are literally moving your entire body weight with each repetition. For this reason, we will use a method called *ladders* and *pyramids*.

With *ladders* we start by performing just 1 repetition, take 3 deep breaths, then perform 2 repetitions. Take 4 or more deep breaths, then perform 3 pull-ups, and so on. Stop when you get to the point where you can only squeeze out one additional rep. Then move to the next variation of pull-ups. On paper, this ladder would look like this: 1 + 2 + 3 + 4 = 10 repetitions.

A *pyramid set* is identical to a ladder except that once we reach the top of the ladder we then work our way down. For example, let's say you can work up to 5 repetitions at the top of your ladder. Instead of stopping and moving to the next pull-up variation, we would then work our way down the other way. On paper, this pyramid would look like this: 1 + 2 + 3 + 4 + 5 + 4 + 3 + 2 +1 = 25 repetitions.

Both ladders and pyramids are wonderful methods to increase your total repetition volume and to dramatically increase your one set maximum. For instance, if you were to perform pyramid sets of 1 to 5 and back down to 1 for all 6 pull-up variations, you would be performing 150 total repetitions. And because you are using so many variations, you would be hitting your muscles from multiple angles and dramatically increase your all-around functional fitness, not to mention your physique.

THE FUREY BRIDGE

Ready

Photo 1 shows your starting position.

Set

From here slowly begin to rise on to your toes while simultaneously moving your forehead closer to the mat.

Go

Ultimately your goal is to reach the point where your nose is touching the mat. Once there, the objective is to hold this isometric/stretch contraction for 3 minutes.

PLEASE NOTE: It may take several months of slow consistent practice to reach a nose-to-mat bridge. Don't worry, there's no rush. It took me several months as well.

TRAINING MEMO: *Men & Women*

While this exercise is incredibly beneficial for athletes, it may be beyond the needs of some people. If that is the case for you, simply perform the neck exercises from Workout #2 as an alternative.

BEHIND THE NECK PULL-UP

Ready

Take a wide grip at least 6" to either side of your shoulders. Grip the bar tightly to activate your entire arm muscle structure.

Set

Slowly start to pull your entire body up and slightly forward of the bar in a smooth motion. Maintain tension in the entire upper back and arm musculature.

Go

At the top of this movement the trapezius muscles of your upper back at the base of your neck will make contact with the bar. Pause for "one tiger one," then reverse direction, continuing a smooth movement.

TRAINING MEMO: *Men & Women*

This is the most difficult of the pull-up variations. Please pay special attention to form. Merely bending and touching the neck is not correct. **REMEMBER:** The shoulder structure is in front of the bar at the top of the movement. Only exceptionally strong and flexible men and women will be able to perform this exercise.

STANDARD WIDE GRIP PULL-UP

Ready

Take a wide grip at least 6" to either side of your shoulders. Grip the bar tightly to activate your entire arm muscle structure.

Set

Slowly pull your entire body smoothly and fluidly to the bar until your chin is above the bar.

Go

At the top of the movement pause for a count of "one tiger one," then slowly lower yourself under full control to the extended arm position.

TRAINING MEMO: *Men & Women*

As with the previous exercise, a slow controlled movement creates maximum results.

STANDARD MARINE PULL-UP

Ready

Start with your arms at shoulder width. Grip the bar tightly and feel the tension in both forearms and upper arms.

Set

Slowly start to pull yourself up to the bar as smoothly as possible while feeling your muscles contracting.

Go

At the top of the movement pause for a count of "one tiger one," then slowly lower yourself under full control to the extended arm position.

TRAINING MEMO: *Men & Women*

This is the standard pull-up used to test the functional upper body strength of the U.S. Marines. Performing 20 consecutive pull-ups earns a perfect score of 100.

CLOSE GRIP PULL-UP

Ready

Grip the bar as shown. Thumbs and index fingers should be touching. Squeeze the bar tightly to activate the entire arm musculature.

Set

Slowly begin pulling yourself up until your chin clears the bar.

Go

At the top of the movement count "one tiger one," consciously tensing the muscles of the arms and upper back. Then slowly lower your body to the extended arm position.

TRAINING MEMO: *Men & Women*

This is an especially powerful movement for the entire arm musculature. Both forearms and upper arms are powerfully contracted in both directions.

CLOSE GRIP CHIN-UP

Ready

This exercise is very similar to the previous exercise except this time your palms are facing toward you. Once again, grip the bar tightly in order to activate the entire arm musculature.

Set

Slowly and smoothly pull yourself up until your chin clears the bar.

Go

At the top of the movement hold for a count of "one tiger one," while powerfully contracting the muscles of the arms and upper back. Then slowly lower your body to the extended arm position.

TRAINING MEMO: *Men & Women*

This version of the "chin-up" works the biceps and forearms intensively. Make sure you perform slow steady repetitions.

COMMANDO PULL-UP

Ready

Study the photo. Note that the palms are staggered and facing each other. Grasp the bar tightly.

Set

Leaning back slightly, begin to slowly pull yourself straight up until your left shoulder touches the bar.

Go

Once your shoulder touches the bar, hold for a count of "one tiger one," then slowly lower your body to the extended arm position. Repeat the entire sequence, touching your right shoulder in the top position. Each complete extension and contraction counts as one repetition.

TRAINING MEMO: *Men & Women*

This is a great exercise for the entire upper body musculature, including the abdominal region.

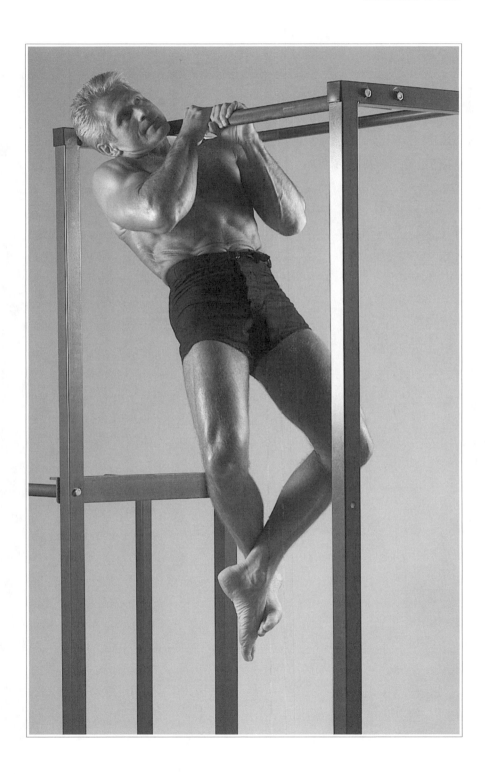

The Miracle**SEVEN**

*Workout***SIX**

Legs

Glutes

Hips

SHAPELY, WELL MUSCLED LEGS
THAT GO THE DISTANCE

Charles Atlas, from MacFadden's *Physical Culture Encyclopedia,* 1938

When you think of perfectly developed athletic legs, what is the first image that comes to mind? Do you think of the legs of a dancer? A martial artist? A soccer player? A world-class cyclist such as Lance Armstrong? Or something entirely different?

As you can see, depending upon who you are, your frame of reference, and your personal athletic interests, your answer could fall anywhere within a wide spectrum of possibilities. Personally, I always wanted to have the lithe, muscular legs of Charles Atlas. Why? Because when I was a little kid I had polio and literally had to spend *years* in the rehabilitation of my legs. Much of that time was spent on crutches, which wasn't all bad because using the crutches helped me develop a powerful set of forearms for a little kid. In fact, my friends all called me "Popeye" because of it.

During those years, I spent several weekends every month at my grandfather's house, and I always went into his personal library and studied his *Physical Culture Encyclopedia* and magazines that were dated from the 1920s to the '40s. I especially liked MacFadden's *Physical Culture* magazines, because they opened up a whole new world of possibilities for me. *Physical Culture* was literally light years ahead of its time with articles not only about physical health and strength but also the whole spectrum of human experience. MacFadden spoke about the development of a positive mental attitude and the power of positive expectations—something the people of

America desperately needed during the Depression of the 1930s…and I needed for my legs.

Bernarr MacFadden at age 70

But of all the articles in those magazines, it was the stories by and about Charles Atlas that always grabbed my attention. This was due in part to the fact that from my earliest recollections I'd been hearing about him from my dad, my grandfather, and my uncles. He was *the man* as far as they were concerned. But there was a particular article from 1936 that really spoke to me. It was written when Charles Atlas was 43 years old, and in it he was outlining his philosophy of total health, strength, and fitness. In the article Mr. Atlas was adamant that his development was the result of his non-apparatus approach. And his physique actually looked better in those photos than it had in articles dating back to the early 1920s. He literally looked much better with age.

It was this article from Charles Atlas that created a dream in me. That dream was not only to develop a lithe, muscular athletic physique like Charles Atlas's, but to be able to run 10 miles in 1 hour (which is exactly what Mr. Atlas stated he had done earlier on the day he wrote the article). When you're a kid on crutches, this is no small dream! I told my grandfather that "Someday I'll run 10 miles just like Charles Atlas." So you can imagine that when my grandfather put me on the Atlas course at the age of 10, I really tore into those leg exercises because I wanted to run like Atlas. The truth is those exercises did me a world of good. By the time I was 12, I had won three blue ribbons in running events in our school's sixth-grade track and field events. They were for the 50-yard hurdles, 50-yard dash, and the 880-yard run. (Twenty-one 12-year-olds started that half-mile race, and three of us finished it.)

But in addition the leg exercises made it much easier for me to excel in the martial arts training that I began in my mid teens. Believe me, I had no problem developing some serious kicking power. I assure you that following these exercises will help develop your legs to your own body's natural perfection. You will simultaneously develop your strength, flexibility, balance, coordination, endurance, speed, and aesthetics. And keep in mind that balance is a critical factor to all-around strength and fitness, particularly as we age.

So let's take a look at seven exercises you can do to enhance not only your leg development but every single component of functional lifelong strength and fitness.

The seven exercises are:

Charles Atlas, from the July 1937 issue of *Physical Culture*

#1—BALANCE SQUAT

#2—SCISSORS SQUAT

#3—HINGES

#4—KNEE PULL IN

#5—KNEE PRESS OUT

#6—LIEDERMAN LEG PRESS OUT

#7—POWER KICKING

BALANCE SQUAT

Ready

Stand erect with your heels together and your toes apart.

Set

Raise high on your toes, flexing the muscles of your entire leg structure.

Go

Slowly descend while maintaining your balance on your toes until you reach the bottom position. Reverse direction and extend to the standing position—remaining on your toes the whole time. As you become adept at this exercise, you may want to vary the speed from time to time.

TRAINING MEMO: *Men & Women*

This variety of the Deep Knee Bend offers a combination of benefits few other exercises can provide. Every attribute of true athletic fitness is enhanced. Charles Atlas recommended that his student do 100 or more of this variation, using as many sets as necessary.

SCISSORS SQUAT

Ready

While standing, cross your legs in front of you in the shape of a scissors and evenly distribute your weight over each foot.

Set

Extend your arms straight in front of you for balance.

Go

While maintaining your back in a straight and upright position, slowly lower your body, bending sideways at the knee. Go as low as is comfortable and then come back up as smoothly as possible. Repeat with opposite leg in front.

TRAINING MEMO: *Men & Women*

This exercise hits the side quadriceps in a way that no other exercise duplicates. Once again, balance, coordination, and muscle control are optimized.

HINGES

Ready

Body in a straight line from knees to head. Beginners should start with hands at waist. Those who are advanced should start with their hands behind their heads.

Set

Feel the tension in your entire body as you powerfully flex your abdominals and glutes.

Go

Slowly lean back, maintaining the tension and control over your entire body. Extend backward only as far as is comfortable and then come forward to an upright position.

TRAINING MEMO: *Men & Women*

I was amazed by how intense the muscle contraction was when performing this exercise. When you get to the point where you are performing sets of 10, you'll be amazed at the results.

Okay, I admit it. I learned this exercise from Wendie Pett. And as so many of you know, her Highness (and I say that respectfully) has been a dancer all her life. Still, up until Wendie taught me this one, I thought I had seen them all. Not so! This exercise will hit your quads and abs (yes, you read that right, your *abs*) in a way that no other exercise does.

KNEE PRESS-IN

Ready

Position yourself in a squatting position, sitting on your heels with your knees wide apart.

Set

Grasp your knees with your hands just inside.

Go

Now try to bring your knees together while resisting powerfully with your hands.

TRAINING MEMO: *Men & Women*

This is a "double duty" exercise. It is superb for your inner thighs, and it is also just as good for your upper back, shoulders, and arms. Practice this one often.

KNEE PRESS-OUT

Ready

Position yourself in a squatting position, sitting on your heels with your knees together.

Set

Grasp your knees with your hands on the outside.

Go

Against powerful resistance, force your knees outward as far as possible.

TRAINING MEMO: *Men & Women*

The benefits you'll reap from this exercise are similar to Exercise #4. You'll feel what I mean when you try it.

LIEDERMAN LEG PRESS OUT

Ready

Grasp your right heel with your right hand exactly as shown.

Set

Against powerful resistance provided by your right arm, slowly extend your right leg as far as possible until your knee is straight.

Go

It's the last part, the straightening of the knee that is most difficult. But keep practicing, it yields exceptional results.

TRAINING MEMO: *Men & Women*

Strength and balance are dramatically enhanced by this exercise. Perform the same number of repetitions on each leg.

POWER KICKING

Ready

Stand on one foot with your arms extended.

Set

Practice kicking your opposite leg as high as you can.

Go

Practice kicking forward, backward, and to the side.

TRAINING MEMO: *Men & Women*

This is a superb exercise for strength, flexibility, balance, speed, coordination, and the athletic look it will bring to your legs.

The Miracle SEVEN

Workout SEVEN

Advanced Level Only

Ultimate Size

Shape on the Hurry Up

ADVANCED LEVEL ONLY—
ULTIMATE SIZE AND SHAPE ON THE HURRY UP

If you look back at Workout #1, you'll recall that Charles Atlas sold his Dynamic Tension Training System in 12 weekly installments, which meant he had to deliver noticeable and exceptional results almost from day one or students would become discouraged and drop out. The truth is that less than 5 percent of his students ever dropped out. And Charles Atlas was charging $35 for his course back in 1929 (the equivalent of $360 today) and throughout the Great Depression. It's also a fact that he and his business partner, Charles Roman, became millionaires during that period of time. Incredible? You better believe it.

I mention this because the cornerstone of the Atlas training method was the Atlas Push-up, which was Exercise #1 of Lesson One, which Mr. Atlas emphatically stated was the single most important exercise of all. The success of the Atlas training method is now a part of American history. And just as the push-up was the king of all exercises back then, make no mistake about it—*it still is king!*

That's why the following training schedule consists entirely of push-ups. And to make our case even stronger, I'm going to share with you what a friend told me back in June 2001. My friend Wayne was suffering from "Busted-Up Weightlifter Syndrome." He called and said, "Hey, John, it turns out you were right all along." I responded, "That's great to hear, but what I was right about?" He said he had read an article in *Iron Man* magazine that verified everything I had been saying since we were in high school together more than 30 years previous.

The push-up was the cornerstone of the Charles Atlas Bodybuilding Course.

I was shocked. Why? Because *Iron Man* magazine is one of the premier bodybuilding magazines that promotes steroids and chemical enhancement and the use of weights. Here is an excerpt from my *Pushing Yourself to Power* book that tells the whole story.

"The concept of doing high volume push-ups every day is not unique to my program. In fact, in the June 2001 issue of *Iron Man* magazine, author Bill Starr wrote an incredible article in which he cited two examples of off-the-charts results that he had personally witnessed from men who used the push-up *alone*. The first was his friend Jack King of Winston-Salem, North Carolina, who was recovering from a near-death experience and found he could no longer do any upper body weight training exercises. By that he meant *none*. No flat benches, inclines, declines—*nothing*. So Mr. Starr said that his friend improvised and did a partial push-up with his feet on a bench and his hands on blocks to take the pain and pressure off his wrists. Slowly but steadily Mr. King worked up to four sets of 150 repetitions. His payoff was rather astounding. Mr. King went on to win several physique contests, including the Masters Mr. America.

"The other example Bill Starr cited was from his Air Force days when he was stationed in Iceland. A young corporal whom Starr knew had allowed himself to get into terrible shape and gained fifty pounds (all of it 'ugly weight'). According to the article, this young man was eligible for a furlough soon and decided he wanted to look his best for his young bride, since he'd only been married a week before shipping off to Iceland. So this guy got his act together and stopped drinking booze and cut way back on his eating. Then he recalled how effective push-ups had been in boot camp, and he decided to go on a push-up blitzing routine.

"But there was a problem. He was in such bad shape that all he could manage was a shaky 15 reps. Nonetheless, with a steely resolve this guy slowly but surely added both repetitions and sets. Starr said that every time he saw the corporal on base, whether in the rec room, the mess hall, or the barracks, he'd drop down and do a set of push-ups. He got to the point where he was cranking out 75 reps per set and completing 20 sets each day for a total of 1,500 reps. Starr said he had never seen anyone transform his body so rapidly and radically as this guy did. After less than one month he had an incredible physique with arms, chest, and shoulders that were truly amazing. As Starr said, *He looked as though he'd been doing advanced level bodybuilding for some time.*"

Earle E. Liederman, King of Mail-Order Bodybuilding during the 1920s, used the push-up extensively.

I could hardly believe Bill Starr's last statement. Why? Because the effectiveness of whatever approach one follows to achieve anything in his or her life is determined by just one thing—RESULTS! If something, anything delivers the most extraordinary results you have ever witnessed, then that something must also be an incredibly amazing and result-producing method. The fact that both men had achieved sensational results following a method that was outside Mr. Starr's normal weight training paradigm does not make it any less effective. To the contrary, I'm amazed that Mr. Starr didn't acknowledge the truth for what it clearly was in both cases. The push-up—an exercise that has been used since the dawn of history to transform and build beautiful physiques, exceptional strength, and superior functional fitness—*is advanced bodybuilding*, when properly applied.

With that in mind, I want to share seven variations of push-ups that can and will help you achieve an exceptional physique, tremendous levels of endurance, strength, and all-around functional fitness.

The seven exercises are:

#1—THE FUREY PUSH-UP
#2—STANDARD LIEDERMAN PUSH-UP
#3—LIEDERMAN FEET ELEVATED PUSH-UP
#4—ATLAS PUSH-UP I
#5—ATLAS PUSH-UP II
#6—HANDSTAND PUSH-UP
#7—EXTENDED RANGE HANDSTAND PUSH-UP

TRAINING NOTES

Although there are seven push-up variations presented here, it is not necessary for you to perform all seven in any given workout. The idea is to give you a wide range of possibilities that allow you to challenge your muscles from a great variety of angles and directions, thus ensuring the utmost in functional strength as well as physique development.

Sets and repetitions are up to you. Many of our Transformetric students perform sets of push-ups throughout the day. And many have exceeded 500 per day and been amazed at the extraordinary changes achieved in development.

Regardless of what variations you employ, always practice flawless form. Maintain tight abs and glutes at all times.

The Handstand Push-up should be attempted by only extraordinarily well-conditioned men and women. I've seen many men who could bench press in excess of 400 pounds who could not perform a single Full Range Standard Handstand Push-up, let alone ever dream of doing the extended range variety. This exercise maximizes your strength-to-body weight ratio. So use extreme care in performing it, and be sure that all breakables are safely out of range.

Carefully review all photos.

Breathe naturally. *Exhale* during the extension movement or time of greatest effort. *Inhale* during the lowering phase.

Actor Woody Strode developed his incredible physique by performing 1,000 push-ups daily.

Herschel Walker performs 1,500 daily push-ups to maintain his incredible physique.

THE FUREY PUSH-UP

Ready

Position your hands on the floor, shoulder-width apart, and head tucked in looking directly at your feet. Your feet will be wider than shoulder-width apart. Legs and back are straight, forming an inverted "V." Your butt is the highest point of your body.

Set

Bending your elbows, begin a smooth circular descent. Almost touch your chest and upper body to the floor as you continue the circular range of motion, arriving at the top with straight arms and looking at the ceiling. Consciously flex your triceps.

Go

Return to the starting position by raising your hips and buttocks while simultaneously pushing back with straight arms until you arrive at the inverted "V." Continue as smoothly and fluidly as possible.

TRAINING MEMO: *Men & Women*

This incredible exercise can be very challenging at first. There are many men who can bench press in excess of 400 pounds who cannot do 25 consecutive Furey Push-ups.

STANDARD LIEDERMAN PUSH-UP

Ready

Begin in arms extended position. Your body forms a straight line from neck to shoulders.

Set

While maintaining tension in your abdominals and lower back to prevent sagging, slowly bend your arms.

Go

Upon arriving at the position shown in the bottom photo, pause for a count of "one tiger one." Then extend to arrive at the top position. All movement in both directions should be smooth.

TRAINING MEMO: *Men & Women*

Many great athletes, including Herschel Walker and Woody Strode, developed extraordinary physiques using this exercise almost exclusively.

LIEDERMAN FEET ELEVATED PUSH-UP

Ready

This is the same as Exercise #2 except your feet are now elevated. The higher the feet the more upper chest and shoulder intensive the exercise becomes.

Set

Always maintain flexed abs when performing this or any push-up variation to protect the lower back.

Go

Upon arriving at the position shown in the bottom photo (be careful about your nose), pause for a count of "one tiger one." Then extend to arrive at the top position. All movement in both directions should be smooth.

TRAINING MEMO: *Men & Women*

Some students get to the point where they can perform sets of 75 or more in this position. However, it is not essential to take this exercise that far.

ATLAS PUSH-UP I

Ready

Place two chairs a comfortable distance apart so your chest can descend to a point lower than your hands. Your arms are in the extended position, abs flexed, and body in a straight line from heels to shoulders.

Set

Slowly descend so that your chest is fully stretched. Do not force yourself to descend beyond what is comfortable. Your range of motion will naturally increase in time.

Go

While maintaining tension throughout the entire body, slowly extend your arms to arrive at the starting position.

TRAINING MEMO: *Men & Women*

This exercise was the foundation upon which the entire Charles Atlas Dynamic Tension Bodybuilding System was built. **DON'T NEGLECT IT.** Results come very quickly when performing this variation.

ATLAS PUSH-UP II

Ready

Performed exactly as the Atlas Push-up I with the exception that your feet are elevated above the hands.

Set

Maintain flexed abs and glutes to protect your lower back. Descend only as far as is comfortable.

Go

While maintaining tension throughout the entire body, slowly extend your arms to arrive at the starting position.

TRAINING MEMO: *Men & Women*

This exercise builds the entire upper body musculature while adding tremendous strength. It changes the emphasis of development from the lower pectoral line to more of the middle pectoral muscles. Especially good for boxers who want to throw a looping overhand right with the kind of power Rocky Marciano had.

HANDSTAND PUSH-UP

*** WARNING: FOR THE VERY ADVANCED TRAINEES ONLY ***

Ready

Place hands slightly wider than shoulder-width apart, approximately 12" to 18" from the wall.

Set

Perform a handstand so that only the bottoms of your feet are touching the wall. Flex your abs and glutes to protect the lower back.

Go

Slowly descend until your nose or chin is within an inch of the floor. Pause for a count of "one tiger one," then slowly push back to full extension maintaining control at all times.

NOTE: After you become proficient at this exercise you may vary hand spacing from very narrow to very wide in order to enhance strength and all-around development.

TRAINING MEMO: *Men & Women*

This exercise utilizes virtually 100 percent of your body weight. Only extremely strong, well-conditioned athletes with superior leverage will be able to practice this exercise. It is important that you use the utmost of care in performing this exercise.

*** WARNING: FOR THE VERY ADVANCED TRAINEES ONLY ***

EXTENDED RANGE
HANDSTAND PUSH-UP

*** WARNING: FOR THE EXTREMEMLY ADVANCED ONLY ***
...unless you have a death wish. But then again there are less painful ways to go besides breaking your neck. –J.P.

Ready

Place your hands at approximately shoulder-width apart on two chairs or boxes of equal height, approximately 12" to 18" from the wall. Be certain that the boxes or chairs are both stable and strong enough to support your entire body weight.

Set

Perform a handstand so that only the bottoms of your feet are touching the wall. Make sure that your abs are tight and legs are straight.

Go

Under complete control bend your elbows slowly and descend slowly until your shoulders are even with your hands. Then reverse direction slowly and push back to complete extension.

TRAINING MEMO: *Men & Women*

This exercise is one of the most difficult exercises in the entire realm of physical culture. To do it even once is a tremendous feat of strength. To do it for repetitions will be in the realm of dreams for all but the very strongest.

*** WARNING: FOR THE EXTREMEMLY ADVANCED ONLY ***

*"Change the way you look at things…
and the things you look at change."*

From the time I was ten years old, I have been amazed by how we can change our world simply by changing our thoughts. For me, it began when I refused to remain a victim to a bully and I said, "I don't want anyone to ever hurt me again." Sharing that thought with my grandfather and Uncle Wally, I was brought face to face with an opportunity to transform myself with the Charles Atlas Training System. Because of that one thought and the desire to take immediate action, my life and destiny were changed forever.

YOU have the power to change your destiny, and it all begins with a single thought and the decision to act upon it. In *The Miracle Seven* you have been taught everything you need to know about the nutrition and exercise that will totally transform your body and your life. You've been given the opportunity to change both your thoughts and the way you look at yourself. You've learned you can become incredibly strong and fit without ever having to rely on anything outside yourself. And you realize that God has blessed you with a body that is the most incredible piece of exercise equipment ever created.

Think about it! What other exercise machine or device allows you to exercise with infinite combinations of variable force and speed from variable angles and positions and with variable ranges of motion? A machine capable of challenging the absolute limits of your strength, flexibility, endurance, balance, speed, coordination, and aesthetics, thus enhancing all seven attributes of true athletic strength and fitness. A machine with a built-in computer complete with its own cooling system that instantly senses changes in heat and energy production throughout your entire body, which automatically adjusts its force and speed to keep you from injuring yourself. A machine that senses sore spots in your body as well as potential points of injury, which will instantly adjust both force and tempo to compensate so you don't aggravate that condition. A machine so portable it literally goes wherever you go, and so compact you can give yourself a complete workout in a very limited space.

Bottom line: No machine or device has ever existed that can help you transform yourself better than the ultimate exercise machine that your Creator blessed you with on the day you were born, and *The Miracle Seven* can serve as your instruction manual to get the most out of it.

It is our hope and prayer that you will take this opportunity for transformation and become the man or woman whom you most certainly can be.

Blessings to you,

John & Wendie

Unleash Your Greatness

AT BRONZE BOW PUBLISHING WE ARE COMMITTED

to helping you achieve your ultimate potential

in functional athletic strength, fitness, natural

muscular development, and all-around superb

health and youthfulness.

Our books, videos, newsletters, Web sites, and training seminars will bring you the very latest in scientifically validated information that has been carefully extracted and compiled from leading scientific, medical, health, nutritional, and fitness journals worldwide.

Our goal is to empower you! To arm you with the best possible knowledge in all facets of strength and personal development so that you can make the right choices that are appropriate for *you*.

Now, as always, **the difference between greatness and mediocrity** begins with a choice. It is said that knowledge is power. But that statement is a half truth. Knowledge is power only when it has been tested, proven, and applied to your life. At that point knowledge becomes wisdom, and in wisdom there truly is *power.* The power to help you choose wisely.

So join us as we bring you the finest in health-building information and natural strength-training strategies to help you reach your ultimate potential.

IF YOU'VE BEEN LOOKING FOR AN EXERCISE SYSTEM that will give you the results you've always dreamed of having, does not require either a gym or expensive exercise equipment, can be done anytime and anyplace without requiring an outrageous commitment of time, you're holding it in your hands.

Based solidly upon the most effective exercise systems as taught by Earle E. Liederman and Charles Atlas during the 1920s, *Pushing Yourself to Power* provides you with everything you need to know to help your body achieve its natural, God-given strength and fitness potential. Whether your desire is simply to slim down and shape up, or to build your maximum all-around functional strength, athletic fitness, and *natural* muscularity, you will find complete training strategies specifically tailored to the achievement of your personal goals.

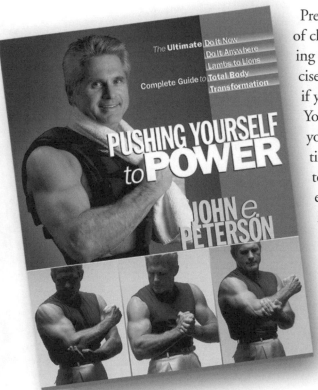

Precisely illustrated with 100s of clear, detailed photos showing every facet of every exercise, you'll never have to guess if you're doing it right again. You'll achieve the stamina you've always wanted in less time than it requires to drive to a gym and change into exercise clothes. Feel what it's like to have twice as much energy as you ever thought you'd have!

THE TRANSFORMETRICS™ TRAINING SYSTEM offers the most honest, straightforward approach to safe, lifelong strength, youthfulness, and long-term fat loss ever created. It is founded on the premise that there are no quick fixes, no magic diets, and nobody has a magic wand to give people the lithe, athletic, sculpted physique they've always dreamed of having. Three things are required: the right balance of nutritious foods, the right strength-building, body-sculpting exercise system, and the knowledge and commitment to put them together.

In the *60 Day Personal Power Health & Fitness Journal,* John and Wendie offer:

• A complete exercise program featuring the Transformetrics™ Training System to help people slim, strengthen, and help their body achieve its natural, God-given strength and fitness potential…without the requirement of a gym or expensive exercise equipment.

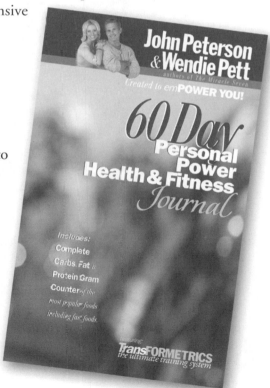

• Complete food charts that feature protein, fat, and carbohydrate grams as well as calories.

• User-friendly exercise charts to help people keep track of their daily progress.

• And inspiring quotes, scriptures, and more to help them stay motivated.

John Peterson & Wendie Pett
authors of *The Miracle Seven*
Created to emPOWER YOU!

60 Day
Personal Power
Health & Fitness
Journal

Includes:
Complete
Carbs, Fat &
Protein Gram
Counter *of the most popular foods including fast foods*

TransFORMETRICS
the ultimate training system

AWESOME STRENGTH AND A GREAT PHYSIQUE
WITHOUT MOVING A MUSCLE

Isometrics, when done correctly, can reshape a person's physique and add strength beyond imagination without the person ever moving a muscle. By powerfully contracting the muscle in an isolation hold, a person can literally sculpt their body, shed fat, and rebuild nerve endings without ever having to go to a gym or lift weights. But the power of isometrics lies in being taught how to do them correctly.

John Peterson, the creator of Transformetrics™ Training System, details the isometric exercises and how he incorporates them into his everyday life. Wendie Pett teaches how certain isometric holds are used to attack those trouble zones that women are especially concerned about.

Available early 2005.

NEW *from* ALAN WATSON

WITH WELL OVER TEN YEARS OF RESEARCH in cardiovascular nutrition, Alan Watson refutes the current medical hypothesis that dietary cholesterol and saturated fat cause heart disease. Rather, he provides compelling historical and scientific evidence that refined sugar, highly processed foods, margarine and shortening (containing dangerous trans fatty acids), and following the nutritional advice from "leading authorities" and "experts" in government and medicine have cost us dearly. Heart-related disease will claim nearly one million lives this year, and one in three children born in the year 2000 will develop diabetes and 80 percent of all diabetics die of heart disease.

21 Days to a Healthy Heart offers a sound perspective on heart health that challenges the status quo opinions in the medical field and dismisses misleading or outdated ideas about heart disease.

Watson demonstrates that low-fat diets increase the risk of heart disease and that most people who die of heart disease have low or average blood cholesterol. He analyzes the role of carbohydrates, fats, and protein in diabetes and heart disease and provides specifics on what to eat and what not to eat for heart health.

A truly one-of-a-kind book on understanding, preventing, and reversing diet-related heart disease.

WHEREVER SHE GOES, VALERIE SAXION constantly hears this complaint: "I can't remember when I last felt good. I'm exhausted and rundown. How can I start to feel good again?" This book is Saxion's response to that question, but it goes far beyond just feeling good. "So why don't you feel *great* all the time?" she asks. "Why are you willing to settle for less than 100 percent?" She then lays out a *Lifelong Plan for Unlimited Energy and Radiant Good Health* to help readers give their bodies the opportunity to start feeling great in four basic steps.

Specifically, Saxion guides her readers into an understanding of how their bodies work, how to stop eating junk food, and the importance of body oxygen, exercise, and water. *Candida*, detoxification, fasting, low thyroid, and weight loss are all covered as well as establishing a perfect diet that is filled with foods that supercharge the mind and body. Nature's prescriptions of vitamins, minerals, and herbs supplement all that she teaches.

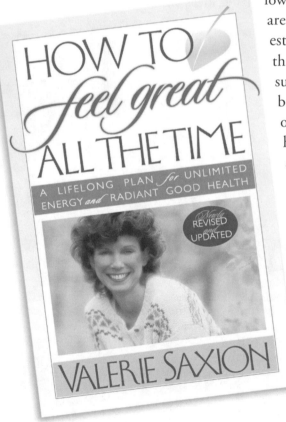

Includes a state-by-state list of more than 800 of America's leading complementary alternative medical doctors.

DO YOU HAVE A CHRONIC HEALTH PROBLEM that you just can shake off? Perhaps you have intestinal problems that come and go? Recurring bouts with diarrhea? Or you're tired all the time and feel depressed? Have you consulted with your doctor but not found an answer? It is very possible that the cause of what you are experiencing is directly due to parasites.

Don't cling to the notion that parasites are limited to the Third World. Parasitic experts estimate that there are between 100 and 130 common parasites being hosted in the American populace today, and a recent health report stated that 85 percent of Americans are infected with parasites. The trick is that the symptoms caused by parasites are subtle because they are experienced commonly by people without parasites, and the vast majority of health-care professionals have little training in diagnosing these masters of disguise and concealment.

If you're alive, you're at risk of this hidden crisis that is damaging millions of people needlessly today. It is a lot easier to become a parasitic host than you think!

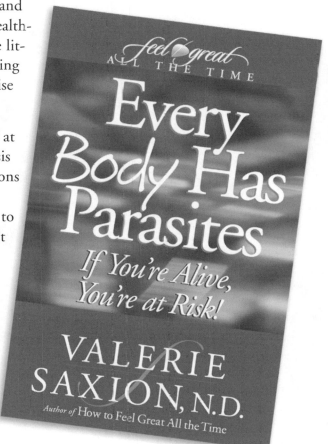

Total Wellness®
Newsletter

Total Wellness, an eight-page, full-color newsletter, is the first wellness newsletter in North America to incorporate *The Total Person Concept*. Their message is that improving lifestyle habits involves setting goals and taking action in *all* areas of life—family and home, financial and career, physical and health, spiritual and ethical, mental and educational, and social and cultural. Their goal is to provide you with an interactive newsletter that motivates you to adopt good lifestyle habits that can make a difference in your overall well-being.

John and I have never seen a more comprehensive newsletter that provides the facts and motivation offered by *Total Wellness*. We are featured monthly columnists in this newsletter, and we invite you to subscribe to *Total Wellness* as an added value for your life! Call 1-800-815-2323, or visit them on the Internet at www.rpublish.com.

John & Wendie
*are Featured
Monthly Columnists*